THE
ANATOMY
OF ANGER

A GIRL'S GUIDE TO LIVING HER
BEST LIFE IN CHRIST

DR. ANTIONETTE D. BROOKINS, LMFT
PH.D IN CHRISTIAN PSYCHOLOGY

ISBN 978-1-0980-2935-7 (paperback)
ISBN 978-1-0980-2936-4 (digital)

Christian Faith Publishing, Inc.
832 Park Avenue
Meadville, PA 16335
www.christianfaithpublishing.com

Printed in the United States of America

CONTENTS

ACKNOWLEDGMENTS

This book was inspired and ordained by Jesus Christ who is at the center stage in my life and was published with the blessings of my family who mean the absolute world to me. The violent details outlined in this book depict a very brief, yet truly impactful transition in my family's life. These graphic scenes of child abuse provide a firsthand view through the lens of a child and my own perspective of my parent's relationship during my early childhood. However brief, these incidents ultimately shaped my view on relationships, love, and my response to anger.

As an adult, I am relieved to have found resolve—to hear my parent's truth and to finally erase false memories about their life together. I gained what I desperately needed as a child; clarity about their brief separation that seemed like a lifetime. My mother shared intimate details regarding her fragile emotional and mental state during this time, and my father expounded on the brief absence that left them both oblivious regarding the mistreatment of their children. I've had the opportunity to sit together with my amazing parents, who continue to be my strength and inspiration. They are #Goals who have endured every hardship and remained committed to their vows after fifty-one years. To God be the Glory! We shared our disappointments, and they shared their apologies for not knowing about the abuse. We all sat saddened and perplexed as we considered how we, I...could be rescued from a life that was never revealed.

Although some issues remain difficult, I know without these hardships, I would not be the woman that I am today, and I bless the Lord who trusted our family enough to endure our season of

5

pain. Through it all, we remain close-knit, steadfast with an unshakable bond! For these hardships give us humility, empathy, and the compassion to do our part to bring healing to a dying nation. This is done through our various ministry endeavors and our collective family ministry, Fields Family Production, LLC.

To my daddy, Vernon Fields, who is the patriarch of the Fields's family, you represent foundation, strength, and resilience. The hardest working man that I know. You gave me a priceless gift, one which none can compare. You introduced me to the lover of my soul, Jesus Christ. No man can hold a candle to you!

To my mom, Ruby Fields, a true woman of God, you continue to be the glue who holds our family together. Your diligence to prayer and the countless hours spent in the throne room on my behalf is inexplicable. Thank you. I am convinced that your prayers and advocacy saved me from the judgment that I certainly deserved but wasn't prepared to serve.

To Butterscotch, Tobaise Brookins, sweet as can be, thank you for loving me like no other man could. You are worth every risk, and you give me the courage to take them all!

To my girlies, Ess, Kaii, and Tai. You give me life, joy, and a residual headache—but this one's for you. Learn from my mistakes and create your own. But these, never duplicate.

To my siblings, Chris, Lena, Vena, and my baby Brother Carlton. Words fail me but look what God has done for us, isn't he amazing? I couldn't imagine life without you guys.

Last but certainly not least, many thanks to my editor, Dr. Chrishele Marshall, who helped my story come to life.

PREFACE

From the looks of things, this girl has it all. She's a senior pastor's wife, business owner extraordinaire, a curator of this, the founder of that, and a sold-out event host with style, personality, and Louboutins to match. I mean, she has it all together, right? Not even!

Sure, my husband is amazing—*most of the time*, my sold-out events are poppin', and I certainly bring new meaning to the word boundaries with my catch phrase "Not it!"

But I would like to let you in on a not so secret. I am literally a hot mess in recovery, and, without the grace of the Father and daily routines, I would still be miserable, emotionally bankrupt, and wallowing in poor self-worth, pity, and doubt. In fact, without Jesus Christ in my life and solid, professional mental health counseling, I am certain that my life would be much different today. I would be either institutionalized or in the state penitentiary.

Hello, my name is First Lady Antionette Denise Brookins, pastor's wife, licensed psychotherapist, and founder of the HolyGhost HomeGirls, LLC, and I am a mean girl.

I wasn't always mean. I certainly was not born a "First Lady" (that was never my dream), and the psychotherapist part, well, that came much later. In fact, before I truly understood the love of Christ and his purpose and will for my life, things were much different.

Let me see if I can paint a picture for you. Imagine you are lost and going through a dark tunnel alone with absolutely no end, light, or hope in sight. It's cold, there are unfamiliar noises, and the stench of death surrounds you. Sometimes you walk, sometimes you run, and every day, you cry. Only, no one hears you. No one is searching for you; in fact, they have no idea you are even missing. I was literally a series of bad decisions, a serial "marry-er" and a bundle of raw, undefined emotions. But God!

Even more significant than how I got out of this mess is how in the world did I find myself in this position to begin with, right? After all, what is a story without all of the grueling details?

Listen, sisters, I invite you to trek with me through this dark tunnel, a thirty-year journey from hurt to healing. A healing found in the most unsuspecting place, in the perfect will of the Father. So, grab a pen, a toasty drink, your favorite notebook, and a box of tissues as I share my untold story and provide you with practical, yet amazingly powerful tools that I have learned along this journey to living my best life in Christ. Are you ready? Let's get started.

INTRODUCTION

The Bible emphatically declares that Christians are to be "angry and sin not" (Eph. 4:26), or is this nothing more than suggestive hyperbole? Doesn't the very idea of suppressing one's anger without retaliation appear oxymoronic? If "no weapon formed against us shall prosper" as the Bible depicts, and if Christians *truly* possess the ability to "do all things through Christ who gives us strength," why does anger remain problematic in the church today?

From the pulpit to the parking lot, anger has become a debilitating cancer to the souls of Christians. A cancer that stunts the spiritual maturation and matriculation of Christians every day. However, the Bible still suggests that Christians possess the ability to be angry and do no harm. I then propose that anger is not the problem. Rather, it is our learned response to anger and untreated emotions that lead to challenges in life and the sin that may follow. This begs the questions, what is anger, what is its origin, and how do we manage it?

1

THE ANATOMY OF ANGER

Caution: Brief explicit language, which may be offensive to some readers.

My relationship with anger began well before I understood who anger was. I chose to personify anger because anger was my friend. In fact, he was my closest friend, almost like a big brother. Anger was my defender, a keeper of dark secrets and my escape. He kept me safe from people and things like nothing or no one else could. Anger allotted me the opportunity to outwardly express things that had been otherwise repressed, held captive, gagged, and bound by chains for the better part of my life. Anger understood me; he did not judge me or attempt to censor me from expressing the savage rage of my life's experiences. Quite the contrary, anger told me that it was okay, that vengeance belonged to me and that all the pain, abuse, disappointment, and fear that I desperately tried to conceal was actually valid. He gave me consent to let it all out in a thunderous roar.

Although there were many significant struggles in my early childhood and adolescence, there are two struggles that are exceptionally noteworthy. First, I grew up black and second, I grew up Christian—Apostolic, to be exact. Now, before you begin to meander down the path of confusion, please allow me to add content to these struggles. You see, everything is about perspective, and perspective is the window through which we view our world.

When I identify black and Christian as struggles, it is because many black Christian families continue to hold on to slave mentality and distorted interpretations of biblical practices.

Although there are many, I chose to outline a few that stand out for me.

1. *Children are to be seen and not heard:*
    "Just sit there and be quiet, you bet not move, don't you make a peep and you bet not embarrass me in front of these folks."

    First of all, seriously? I'm a kid. Nonetheless, perfection was the expectation in the presence of company. We were expected to be on our best behavior and to "speak up" enthusiastically whenever spoken to even though we were forbidden to make a peep. I absolutely agree with the importance of great first impressions. I also agree that we, as parents, should teach our children to be well behaved. My problem was, I was often afraid. I was a very anxious child struggling with what I now understand to be undiagnosed posttraumatic stress disorder (PTSD) and separation anxiety.

    Because of the abuse, I was quite leery of people and, if I'm being honest, sometimes people just looked ugly to me. I'm not sure if this was an early indication of my ability to discern spirits. But I do know that they just didn't look right. Sometimes, I was guarded because that person had already hurt me, while another may have made it a habit to ridicule me. Therefore, the expectation to be nice while adults hugged, gave me suga', and prodded me was repulsive at times. No, they weren't all abusive or inappropriate. But the fact that I had no choice in the matter made me angry. There were other times when grown folks would highlight the very thing that I hated about myself. I was already embarrassed about my short, plaited hair so why did they have to mention it and why did I have to stand there with a plastered-on smile during their discourse?

My hair certainly wasn't my crown and glory. Instead, it was a continued source of agony. My daddy hated my hair and so did I. "Fuzzy Wuzzy was a bear Fuzzy Wuzzy had no hair." This chant is branded forever into my psyche because he chanted it every single day; at least that's the way I remember it. Since I was not allowed to have an opinion about my hair nor given any options of how it was styled, I found no pleasure in saying hello or performing for company. Instead, I just wanted to run away, hide, go play, or my mother to hold me.

Of course, I knew that I was "too big to be carried" and that I was old enough to "stand up straight, be still, stop fidgeting so much, and keep my shirt out my mouth." But being under my mom and hiding my face in her body made me feel safe. And when she wasn't there, I cried or just pretended to be mad all the time. At least then, my bald head and why my hair wouldn't grow wasn't the topic of the conversation.

Often, children are not given the opportunity to have an opinion, especially one that champions an opposing view. When kids act out, they are just "bad, hardheaded" and sometimes "crazy." The fact that I had *many* opinions, an eclectic personality, and mannerisms that were different than any of my siblings didn't make me unique. It made me "a silly child."

2. *Spare the rod, spoil the child:*

I have scoured the Bible and completely exhausted Google, and I have not found this scripture anywhere. "Thus spare the rod, spoil the child" appears to be nothing more than an old adage and a loose interpretation of Proverbs 13:24 that reads, "He that spareth his rod hateth his son: but he that loveth him chasteneth him betimes," and perhaps Proverbs 23:13–14, which says, "Withhold not correction from the child: for if thou beatest him with the rod, he shall not die" (KJV).

I make no claims to be a theologian. And I am but a novice when it comes to exegesis of the Bible. What I can attest to is, that after consultation with great scholars, I have learned that words and phrases used in the Bible require a combination of spiritual illumination and thorough review of context, including geographical location. I also learned that certain scriptures are metaphorical. I would like to say that I am not making any claims or offering any opinion as to whether parents should spank their child(ren). I choose to hold my peace on that topic. However, I do believe that it is of the utmost importance to exercise wisdom, patience, self-control, and compassion when we are training our children.

According to an article in the *New York Times* written by Dr. Stacey Patton, an assistant professor of multimedia journalism at Morgan State University and the author of the forthcoming *Spare the Kids: Why Whupping Children Won't Save Black America*, stated that:

Today, despite 50 years' worth of research on the harms of "tough love" parenting, many black parents still see a slap across the behind or a firm pop on the hand as within bounds. But it doesn't stop there: Statistics gathered by the National Child Abuse and Neglect Data System consistently show that black children are mistreated and killed by their family members at significantly higher rates than children of any other group. Between 2006 and 2015, more than 3,600 black children were killed as a result of maltreatment, according to the Administration for Children and Families. That's an average of 360 children a year, three times higher than other racial and ethnic groups (SR10).

3. *Slave mentality/Slave talk:*

"I will beat cha' 'til the blood run down! Have you lost your cotton-picking mind? I will beat the black off of you! I will slap you into next year. I will slap you into kingdom come" (By the way, I still have no idea where that place is.)

Perhaps the fact that my grandmother was the daughter of a sharecropper was her rationale for how she treated us. In her later years, age had played my grandmother a much gentler hand. She had become the sweet, affectionate, great- and great-great grandmother to our children. The abusive grandmother that my siblings and I knew and feared had become no more than old wives' tales. They could not imagine that the animated, beautiful, blue-eyed, silver-haired woman with a love for money and dancing was anything other than "Granny Goose." One who sang lullabies that you don't find in the books of nursery rhymes.

It was during these final years of her life that I was able to have candid conversations with her about the abuse, about the trauma, and about her own life. I was finally able to ask her the one question that haunted me for decades. "Why?" Her response, although simplistic, was honest. It was her truth, and it freed me from years of pain and the implicit hatred that had taken residence in my heart. "I did the best that I knew how." As her steel blue eyes stared straight ahead and a solitary tear strolled down her chiseled face, I understood.

This was clearly a perpetuation of abuse that had been passed down through hundreds of generations, dated back to the plantation where abuse at the hands of slave masters was a way of life. Frederick Douglas, a former slave, an abolitionist and one of the most prolific African American writers in American history, has given account of his life as a slave. As he recorded in many of his writings, he saw the "brutality of slavery on full display." His owner and overseer, Aaron Anthony, fed slave children from troughs and mercilessly whipped slaves who did not obey his orders

15

quickly enough. "The young, the old; no one was exempt." This single quote from *Life and Times of Frederick Douglass: His Early Life as a Slave, His Escape from Bondage, and His Complete History to the Present Time* (the electronic copy, 1999) provides context to my entire childhood. According to the social learning theory, which will be discussed later, children naturally repeat what is consistently modeled for them. So it's clear to me why my grandmother continued the cycle of verbal and physical abuse that she was exposed to as a child.

4. *When you have a problem, you talk to God (pray) about it. When problems are really bad, you fast. When things are severe, you talk to your pastor.*

Okay, I admit that this sounds preposterous when written here in black and white, because of the notion that the pastor is portrayed as the almighty fixer of all things broken. But for many black Christian families, this was a way of life. Professional mental health counseling wasn't even an option. As I think about it, it was never mentioned. Who could afford counseling anyway? Was that even something that was offered to children in the hood in the 1970s and '80s? All I knew is what I had been told. "Jesus is the wonderful counselor" (and he is) and that we should "cast all of our cares on him" (and we should), that "the prayers of the righteous availaeth much and heals the sick." My question is, "If Jesus was the wonderful counselor, does that make the pastor his resident intern despite his inability to provide effective mental health counseling?"

Remember, I said I am a pastor's wife, so I know first-hand the wisdom, dedication, and anointing that the man or woman of God has been given to provide wise counsel. I also know that there is wisdom in knowing when to refer. Even as a pastor's wife myself and licensed psychotherapist, there are times when situations are within my scope of practice (meaning, I am licensed to be able to treat someone), but it is outside of my scope of competence (meaning, I have no earthly idea what I'm supposed to do with that). It means that a referral is in order.

When I was growing up in holiness, there were no referrals to outside agencies. To even consider a deviation from the process of prayer, fasting and speaking to your pastor meant you had lack of faith. Lack of faith was due to carnality, and carnality meant that your Holy Ghost was under investigation. Unfortunately, this caused people to either back slide and pick up a bottle, the pipe, or a side chick in order to cope or they became great pretenders and "shouted" through the pain. Even as I script this page, I see why I got popped often. It was because I've always had questions and, in black church culture, that was considered rebellion.

I have always been sassy, demonstrative, and full of untamed personality. Unfortunately, this is a part of me that has been marred and diminished due to abuse. Today, as I become more aware of who I am in Christ, I no longer offer apologies for my personality because I now understand that this is how my Father (in heaven) designed me, and it serves me well as a psychotherapist with a trained eye for asking tough questions. The Lord does all things well!

Although my story is painful, riddled with ridicule, envy and doubt, it is integral to the anatomy of my anger, germane to this topic and must be exposed. Mainly due to the fact that silence and covering abuse only adds to the perpetuation of abuse, which leads to anger, anguish, and, in far too many cases, death.

My siblings and I were partially raised by our maternal grandmother, and this is where the majority and the most severe abuse occurred. My dad, although stern and emotionally unaware, was not physically abusive to his children. He really is an awesome man, but I will talk to you about my daddy a bit more as this story unfolds. When it comes to my mom, as silly as this may sound, I deserved every *single* whoopin' that she handed out. Well, except for the one and only time that she slapped me because she thought I called my sister the B word. My mother was always a sweet woman and would bend over backwards for almost anyone. Quite similar to my personal parenting style, she would offer chance after chance and typically only threaten a whoopin' as a last resort. And, in congruence with the adolescent that I was, I often pushed the limits and that's when the problem occurred. She would reach for the closest thing available, typically a belt, a shoe, or in dire straits, a telephone cord as a way to discipline us.

I almost felt sorry for my mother. Even then I could discern the sadness, frustration, and disappointment in her screeching voice, as she yelled out with each swing, "Didn't-I-Tell-You…" followed by, "This hurts me more than it hurts you." Although I did not fully understand it then, the psychotherapist in me is now able to recognize that my mom was codependent. In those times, she had reached her capacity and her failure to set appropriate boundaries with her children and apply natural logical consequences for misbehavior lent way to her naturally falling prey to her own default. This was the propensity to utilize abusive methods that she learned from her own mother.

Whether it was spilling the prune juice, wetting the bed, failing to "clean our plate" (eating our food until every morsel was gone) or not tattling on a sibling, the beatings from my grandmother were frequent and severe. I wonder why Child Protective Services (CPS) was not aware of what was happening to us? Sometimes, I still have flashbacks of a particularly vicious beating my younger sister received when she was probably about five years old. Grandma was teaching her to tie her shoe. I can smell the furnace, hear the creek of the old wooden floors and the whistle of the cord as it whipped through the air. I also see my sister's tiny body shaking, gasping to catch her breath, and writhing with pain while novice, trembling fingers tried to execute the task. As my sister leaned forward, barely able to stand, Grandma swung that cord over her bleeding back. I remember feeling so helpless.

I was only about seven years old. I can't recall if I prayed or stood in silence while my sister was being tortured, but what I do recollect is that I ran to tie her shoe the moment that Grandma left the room. As she took a break to rest from the stress caused by the constant jerking of her whipping arm, I frantically tried to rescue my sister. I always wanted to protect her, but I didn't know how to protect my sister from Grandma. I could see the pain in her eyes, and I just wanted to run away with her to go find our mom. Why would she leave us there? She had to know how Grandma treated us. My attempt to save my sister ended up being a nearly grave mistake—a mistake that is forever branded in my mind. When Grandma returned, my sister received a more severe beating for tying her shoe outside of my grandmother's presence.

I recently spoke to my parents about this incident. First, the room fell silent followed by a sincere, "I had no idea. I would not have allowed this." One thing about being an adult is finally having the ability to have candid conversations, gaining clarity, and finally hearing their truth.

I don't recall when the enuresis began for me, but I do distinctively recall being beat, punched, and jerked into consciousness by the sting of the lacerating "straup." "Get up! I said get up and change these sheets! I will beat cha' til you pee like a pole cat!" It wasn't until I was in junior high school that I decided to check the encyclopedia for the definition. A pole cat, although now considered a dated term and the definition obsolete, pees every few minutes. I was always getting into trouble for something, and "cutting my eyes" was a chronic offense. No, I wasn't a glutton for punishment. It was very difficult to avoid doing so. The expectation was to look straight ahead and directly into an adult's eyes, while they corrected you. While this may sound simplistic enough, there were several factors that made this nearly impossible.

1. An adult was often yelling in close proximity to my face, which made it difficult to remain still and focused.
2. I was not allowed to blink, which caused my eyes to water and burn.
3. I could not smirk, appear annoyed (children were too young to be annoyed), or suck teeth.

4. I could not look away, *ever*, not even for a moment. To do so was considered disrespectful and was an indicator that I was not listening or had little regard for what was being said.

I recall the many times that anxiety brewed in my belly knowing that the punishment for violating any of the aforementioned rules was a swift, instinctive pop, a never-ending lecture or nonstop conversations between the adults about how Nett "just refuses to listen" and how they had "no idea what to do with that child." And in the instance that I did get popped, I dare not bring attention to myself or appear to be injured by the pop. To do so meant that I would receive "something to cry about." Although if I did not appear to be injured to some degree, I was being a "stubborn, rebellious child who had not learned her lesson." So, of course, the threat of a more severe punishment would follow.

While a part of me shudders at the memories, another part of me seriously cannot keep from laughing because this was once considered effective parenting. By now, it may be evident that the anatomy of anger is quite complex and multifaceted. It is not enough for one to say that they are angry, because that is only the tip of the iceberg.

Anger is a secondary emotion, meaning that there are other emotions that come before anger shows up on the scene. As I mentioned earlier in this chapter, anger is a big brother, a friend who protects you from exposing all the other emotions that can render you powerless.

Remember when I said that perception is the window through which we view the world? Well, here is a perfect example and a good place to begin taking notes.

1. *Anger is often easier for someone to express than the other emotions.*
   Anger distracts from primary emotions such as sadness, disappointment, guilt, embarrassment, etc. Primary emotions are perceived by some as a sign of weakness, one that can leave us vulnerable. Thus, for most people, it is difficult to deter-

mine what we are feeling, and anger becomes the likely suspect. We tend to blame anger when there is another emotion lurking underneath or hiding behind her big brother.

When I was being called a bald-headed Fuzzy Wuzzy, I wasn't angry, at least not at first. I was embarrassed because my hair was short. I was humiliated, hurt, and confused because Daddy introduced that chant, and I couldn't understand why he wanted me to feel internal pain. I was frustrated because no matter how much grease I applied to my hair and no matter how much I tried to stretch it with the pressing comb, it never looked any longer, and it certainly never grew.

I have designed two activities or exercises that I use whenever I am teaching clients how to identify primary emotions.

Activity 1:

Grab a large sheet of paper and ask participants to write down all the words that they use to say that they are angry. For example, mad, peeved, pissed, etc. Once they have fully exhausted their vocabulary for words that are synonymous for anger, I inform them that I will strip those words from their vocabulary. This forces them to at least consider other emotions besides anger that they may be feeling.

Activity 2:

I offer a scenario similar to the following:

What if your significant other charged into this room, he began yelling at you in front of this entire class of people, he began to tell you how stupid you are and how you are a lazy, unfit mother who always leaves the kids with someone else.

I then ask them how they would feel.

While most participants defer to default by saying that they are "mad or pissed," I remind them of activity one and begin to explore things a bit further. With some prompt-ing, they become more aware and are able to acknowledge that emotions such as shock, embarrassment, disrespect, fear, and even guilt are more appropriate and more accurate than the scapegoat, anger. It is important to identify and address our primary emotions so that our emotions can be properly cared for. This means we need to talk things through and put interventions into place until the issues are no longer problematic for us. This does not mean that you won't ever feel these emotions again. It simply means that, if dealt with properly, it is less likely that our emotions will disrupt our life.

As we consider perception, we can't allow others to believe that we are weak or that they possess the ability to hurt us. To do so gives credence to further attack, right? *Wrong!* This skewed perception about our emotions keeps us in a place of hostility. Pent-up emotions lead to both physical and emotional problems including irritability, aggression, stress, anxiety, depression, heart disease, etc. Being honest about our emotions does not give others ammunition to hurt us. Honesty helps us to foster more authentic relationships. If someone is using our choice to be honest about our emotions to deliberately hurt us, it is time for us to make a choice about whether we should allow them a place in our life.

2. *Anger is an indicator that you believe you are being violated in some way.*

Whether you are being violated or not, it still deserves some attention. Remember, this is about perception. Especially since anger is often associated with aggression.

Before we go any further, it is important to under-stand that there is a distinct difference between anger and aggression. Don't worry, we will continue to discuss per-ception in subsequent chapters.

Anger is an emotion, what we feel. Aggression is a behavior, what we do in response to feeling anger. Anger is a natural response to stimuli or an activating event. "When you get angry, it is because you have encountered an event in your life that has provoked your anger. Many times, specific events touch on sensitive areas" (Substance Abuse and Mental Health Services Administration 9).

According to SAMHSA, anger is a habitual, learned response:

Anger can become a routine, familiar, and predictable response to a variety of situations. When anger is displayed frequently and aggressively, it can become a maladaptive habit. A habit, by definition, means performing behaviors automatically, over and over again, without thinking. The frequent and aggressive expression of anger can be viewed as a maladaptive habit because it results in negative consequences (6).

Remember the patterns that I mentioned earlier on? Aggression was one of the first maladaptive habits that I adopted in my childhood. I grew up in a home where domestic violence occurred often. Although my older siblings have a much different recollection of these events and recent conversations with my parents also refuted this, I only recall my father coming home drunk and fighting my mother.

You see, I recall pictures falling from the wall, loud noises, and my mother crying on the other side of our adjacent wall. Although I attempted to run to her rescue many times, I was always redirected and banned to my room as the nightmare continued. It's important to note that I could not see what was happening on the opposite side of the wall, and I never once saw my father strike my mother. I do recall being terrified as my undeveloped imagination ran wild. Becoming a codependent savior was another maladaptive pattern that I picked up. I have a lot more to say about this as I unpack my story.

I'm not sure which impacted me more: seeing my parents' fence in the backyard with a bed rail and a hole post digger or hearing my mother yell while I laid dry towels on urine-soaked sheets. While the nickname sounds endearing, "Netsy Wetsy" was far from sweet.

Here's another noteworthy nugget: *Young children often lack the ability to properly differentiate between their imagination and reality. Therefore, it is important to be open about arguments that our children may have overheard. This helps to assure our children that things are okay and minimize the propensity for excessive worry, or worse holding false assumptions that incite terror.*

I learned to abuse myself early on. No, I wasn't cutting or physically injuring myself. Truthfully, back then, I had never heard of anyone doing something like that. Even if I had, I was clever enough to know that doing so would only intensify my problems. Not only would I have been labeled a crazy child, but I would have gotten my tail beat. Although most couldn't recognize it, I abused myself daily with self-deprecating language. I was overly critical of myself and downright mean. I was a self bully! I called myself names such as ugly, worthless, boney, and stupid. Although I didn't want to believe these things about myself, I did. And in the rare case that I mustered up enough self-confidence to counter my beliefs, the kids at school reminded me of my truth.

The smile that I once bore diminished as I learned to instinctively drop my head and conceal teeth that seemed too large for my protruding lips. All of these awkward features were coupled with the fact that I wore long skirts every day. As if my life weren't already complicated enough, I had just gained an all access membership to the social rejects club.

Brutal, right? Just wait, it gets even better. I hadn't even hit high school yet.

Anger is a natural, God-given emotion that is very useful when used appropriately. And anger can be kind enough to provide cues to let us know that something isn't quite right. It is then up to us to use logic and our transformed minds to make a healthy decision about how to respond appropriately to whatever we may be feeling. Just like when we need to relieve ourselves (use the rest room), our body sends a very clear message that we are angry and that we need to respond right away. Failure to do so may result in a potentially embarrassing or, in the case of anger, dangerous situation. These anger cues are divided into four categories: *physical, behavioral, emotional, and cognitive.*

Physiological Components to Anger

Physiological or physical cues refer to the way that our body physically responds to the emotion of anger. For example, when we get upset, our hearts may race, our palms may become clammy and sweaty, our breathing may become shallower, and some even say that the hairs on the back of our necks stand up. On my journey to emotional recovery, I have made a point to become very self-aware of my physiological cues, and I have made a commitment to remain honest with myself as it relates to what I can and cannot tolerate in my life.

Knowing this is helpful for me because they remind me to stop and consider that I want to:

1. Preserve public safety.
2. Continue to protect the woman that I have worked diligently to know and finally learn to love.
3. Preserve my commitment to remain on the visitor check-in side of the state penitentiary.

Over time, I have learned to acknowledge my personal anger cues and to protect my emotions like an infant. When we consider the delicacy of an infant, we know that they need extra care, attention, nurture, and, most of all, protection to mature and survive. Now I am able to give voice to my emotions and easily recognize my anger cues *before* big brother shows up in straight beast mode! I am able to self-regulate, stop, and check in with my inner self. I ask myself, "Why is my tummy churning right now, why do I feel my eyes burning, why do I feel like crying, why is my heart racing… Nett, what's happening here?"

Behavioral Components to Anger

This refers to what we *do* when we are angry. For example, pace, yell, curse, fight, give dirty looks, or threaten to lay our Holy Ghost down.

Personally speaking, my anger shows up like a hurricane, demolishing everything in sight. Once I have fully unleashed my fury, it is very difficult to reign him back in. Remember, he is a friend, big brother, and protector so he shows up in straight defense mode. It is not by happenstance that my anger has a male persona. Whenever I watched love stories or an after-school special, there was often a main character, mainly female, with a protector who was always male. Whether he was a father, a lover, or a big brother, he would step in and save the day. As I further consider this, even fairy tales had a prince charming who whisked the young damsel away, trotting off to the land of happily ever after. Right or wrong, the idea of men being saviors still hold true for me.

By allowing anger to have free reign in my life, I have found myself in many precarious situations. The most severe was when someone attempted to throw me out of a window. Before I explain, let me first say that violence is never ever okay and abuse, in any form, should never be condoned.

So that we are clear about this, I will interject the anger rules and types of abuse:

1. The anger rules are what we should and should not do when we are feeling angry.

2. Types of abuse are the ways in which we cause damage or harm often as a result of feeling anger. See the table below (Sheppard 8):

Table 1. Anger Rules and Types of Abuse

Anger Rules	Types of Abuse
1. Don't Hurt Yourself	1. Verbal
2. Don't Hurt Others	2. Emotional
3. Don't Hurt Property	3. Physical
4. Do Talk About it.	4. Sexual

Source: Sheppard, Tony, L. *Parent Guide to the Anger Thermometer & the Anger Rules*, Groupworks, Inc., 2016.

Now, back to my story. There are specific cases where we have a choice to defuse a potentially hostile situation, avoid a situation, or escape a situation. This is where the preacher says, "I'm going to talk about me, so that I don't have to talk about you."

Ttoni was nineteen years old and living hundreds of miles away from home. I could turn a head regardless of age, ethnicity, culture, social class or economic status, and I knew it. Being externally beautiful on the outside was a skill that I mastered even while being completely shattered and insecure on the inside. I was a beautiful mess.

I was smart, haughty, opinionated, and I made a point to never be censored again. I said what I wanted, whenever and however I chose. I was no longer a scared and emotionally marred seven-year-old. I was in many ways worse. I was a young woman with everything to prove; a girl with an axe to grind.

I can still taste the words as they rolled off of my tongue. "I ain't the bitch that had your sorry ass." Consequently, I can also feel the heat and hear the creek of that old window frame against my back as my friends pled my case. I would like to say that was the last time that this mouth of mine wrote a ticket that my behind could not cash. But unfortunately, I must admit, that's another girl's story.

I already know, before you say it, that *mere* words do not cause or give license for anyone to put their hands on you. But I also know that I could have walked away unscathed, with partial dignity intact had I made another decision that day and walked away from someone who intentionally caused me pain.

Emotional Components to Anger

This refers to how you feel emotionally about the situation that led to anger. If you recall, anger is a secondary emotion; therefore, other emotions are often ignored, diminished or mistaken altogether. This was an eye-opener for me. Learning about the emotional cues of anger offered a new perspective as it related to managing my personal anger. This new perspective continues to help me to stabilize my emotions and think rationally about my choices. So, now instead of hitting, breaking dishes, or shaving my head in an erratic emotional frenzy, I can articulate that I am more than angry. I have the ego-strength and the vocabulary to say that an extramarital affair is both painful and confusing, and that the betrayal of the affair exceeds my capacity to cope. I can then decide if I want to seek professional help, walk away or both. This is a skill that may have saved me from a five-day stay at the county jail.

Cognitive Components to Anger

This refers to the things that are going through your mind whenever you are angry. These are messages that you tell yourself about the situation that caused you to feel angry. I have learned the hard way that negative self-talk can and will intensify the issue. And by now, you know that I have a story for this, too.

It was 1994 in Susanville, California, just a few months before I married my first Was-band. I was a student at a local junior college and part of the Job Corps program. I decided to go off campus on an evening pass to spend time with a girlfriend of mine who had her own apartment about a half mile up the hill. We ended up meeting with my ex, I'll call him Jake to protect the guilty. I can't recall, for the life of me, what we were arguing about. But remember, I was a feisty, hotheaded young woman so trust me when I say, it didn't really take much for me to fly off the handle. As the story goes, I was upset and wanted him to leave. I didn't care that he had traveled thirty miles to see me, and it was of no concern to me that it was now very dark outside, close to curfew, and that he was my only ride back down the hill. I demanded that he leave, and he did just that.

With less than an hour before curfew, I began walking frantically down the hill. Picture this: It's completely dark, I'm afraid that I am in danger of being coyote food, and I'm mad enough to blow a head gasket. As other students are whizzing by in their cars, also rushing to make curfew, several people stopped to offer me a ride. Now, I am almost embarrassed about my response, but the truth shall make us free, right? "Nope! I do not want a ride because I want to be good and mad by the time I get down this hill."

Yikes! So, track with me, ladies, I was:

1. Upset, about God knows what
2. Tired
3. Afraid

4. Alone with my irrational and negative thoughts
5. And I am rehearsing angry responses aloud. Thoughts like, he got me messed up! I can't believe he left me!

Can we all agree that this is a five-star recipe for disaster?

Although I demanded that he leave, and I can be quite convincing, I was also hurt, disappointed, and confused that he actually left me. Everything in me was screaming for help and the need to be held. Why didn't he just hold me and tell me that everything was okay and that he had no desire nor intent to leave? Why didn't he have the power to read my mind?

I now understand why Paul admonishes us in Philippians 4:8 to "think on these things." "Finally brethren whatsoever things are true, whatsoever things are honest, whatsoever things are of good report; if there be any virtue, and if there be any praise, think on these things." Boy, I tell you that the Word of God is the absolute truth, and Paul was spitting game!

To sum things up:

1. Anger is normal, natural, and, when exercised appropriately, healthy.
2. Anger is often the manifestation of other emotions that are too afraid to speak up.
3. Anger sends cues, which are vital to the proper management of our anger. This is our internal check engine light that lets us know that maintenance may be required before we blow a head gasket.
4. When anger shows up, he is asking two questions.

Now please forgive me, I was raised in the ghetto, so "Hood" is my first language. So, allow me to break this down the way that it naturally comes to my mind. For the intellectuals reading this, don't get nervous, I have a degree and I am coming for you next.

When we are faced with an issue, anger comes checking for his sister like, "Sis, we good? You need me to handle this, 'cause we can tear up this whole room and, if things get too heavy, we can always break."

Intellectually stated, "Antionette, something isn't quite right, and I don't like how this is going. Are we in a life-threatening situation here? If so, let's look for the closest exit. But if it comes down to it, we are prepared to fight. Fight or flight."

2

Exploring the Woman of Faith

What She's Made of

As I reflect on my early Christian experience, my concept of God was one of an attention-seeking, overly protective father who lacked compassion. In fact, due to the exhaustive list of "thou shall nots," I ran away from God and gravitated toward other things that seemed to serve me better. It didn't take long for running to become a frequent pattern in my life—a pattern that I will continue to unfold chapter by chapter throughout this book. If professional counseling had been an option for our Christian family back then, I may have been a more evolved woman today. Unfortunately, the fact that we did not have the resources to seek counseling left this black Christian girl without any practical means to deal with her evolving, or dissolving, sense of self.

Have you ever considered what it means to be a woman of faith? I mean really considered the differences between a woman of faith versus the "average" woman. If you haven't, take a few moments now to really give this some thought. Resist the urge to skip to the section where I answer this question for you. We're so lazy as Christians that we often wait for the preacher to tell us who and whose we are instead of going to the source. The Bible invites us to study to show ourselves approved. But I'm certainly not judging you, because I have no stones to throw.

I'm guilty of this myself. I will do a Google search in a minute and declare it a word from the Lord. Like "whoa that's deep" only to be immediately arrested by the spirit who says, "Check the source," which sends me back to the Word of God. The problem is, however, that we don't know how many hands have touched that word and how diluted or polluted it has become since it was lifted from the pages of the Bible.

The simple answer is, a woman of faith is a woman who knows who and whose she is. She is no ordinary woman. She is a woman uniquely crafted by God. She knows that God is not only her savior, but that he's the one who graciously steps into the mess that she has made of her life. She also accepts Jesus Christ as her Lord, the one who reigns supreme and governs her thoughts, actions and, yes, even her relationships. That means that God has her whole heart and every single emotion. Once she has gained a relationship with the Father, she trusts him to become her consultant. She seeks him in every aspect of her life, the good, the bad, and even the ugly, dirty, and embarrassing parts. The downright grimy areas that she doesn't even want God to see. That last part is laughable right, since God is both omniscient and omnipresent? He sees all, knows all, and is in all places, at all times. So, nothing escapes him. But that does not stop our futile attempts to hide things from God.

When we do that, we prohibit God from stepping into our situation and handling the things that are out of our control. It seems that we would rather insult his sovereignty by deducing him to one who simply pays our bills, fixes our credit, blesses us with the car of our dreams, or a husband with a six-figure income. Those things are nice, and he can certainly do that. But if we are honest, these are things that diligence in our finances, good credit, and an attitude adjustment can also do. God wants us to honor him and grant him access to our lives, not strip us of our will and desires. Our free will is the one thing that makes us uniquely human.

Psalm 8:4–9 reads:

> What is mankind that you are mindful of them, human beings that you care for them? You have made them a little lower than the angels and

> crowned them with glory and honor. You made
> them rulers over the works of your hands; you
> put everything under their feet: all flocks and
> herds, and the animals of the wild, the birds in
> the sky, and the fish in the sea, all that swim the
> paths of the seas. Lord, our Lord, how majestic is
> your name in all the earth! (NIV).

This was the angels speaking to God about us. Our God is so much bigger than material things. We serve the omnipotent God who can do what no other power can do.

Jeremiah 32:17 reads:

> Ah, Sovereign LORD, you have made the
> heavens and the earth by your great power and
> outstretched arm. Nothing is too hard for you.
> "I am the LORD, the God of all the people of the
> world. Is anything too hard for me?"

Why not challenge the Lord to handle the things that are out of our control? Things that only he can do such as release us from the bondage of cyclic sins, addictions, strongholds, and generational curses that continue to plague and destroy our lives? These are the things that our God specializes in.

In essence, the difference between the average woman and a woman of faith is that we operate in the supernatural. We no longer have to succumb to our default—the people we naturally are, our savage, presalvation selves commonly known as the "carnal man." This is the girl inside who operates solely on id, "the one of the three divisions of the psyche in psychoanalytic theory that is completely unconscious and is the source of psychic energy derived from instinctual needs and drives" (Id). And boy is our default dangerous! Let me speak for myself. My default is gangsta, and she kept me in trouble. Because of my background, I always had a response. *Always*! And as I mentioned earlier, I have encountered near-death experiences because of it.

Christian Coping Skills

Romans 8:6 warns us against deferring to our default, carnal personas. "For to be carnally minded is death, but to be spiritually minded is life and peace." A woman of faith remembers that she needs a God and that she should not rely on her own strength, natural resources, or degrees. Rather, these things should be supplemental to her supernatural gifts and talents. The woman of faith behaves in a manner that is evident of a sanctified life set apart for the Master's use and for his good pleasure. So instead of giving someone "a piece of our mind," we should respond with a renewed, transformed mind that reflects the love of Christ rather than the fullness of our wrath. If you think I am going to simply throw a slew of Bible verses at you, think again. I gotchu, sis! This is where things become practical, and it's the perfect time to introduce what I have coined "Christian coping skills," which are the basic fundamentals for living our best life in Christ.

1. Prayer
2. Fasting
3. Reading the Bible
4. Communion of the saints

The Bible admonishes us to do these things in order to live a faithful Christian life. These four fundamental concepts have been a lifesaver, and I don't mean that figuratively. These coping skills have literally saved my life. It's a shame that I didn't utilize them earlier. But if I had, I probably wouldn't be writing this book. And trust me when I say that my process, my struggle, my journey to healing has blessed thousands of women. And for that, I say thank you, Father. It was worth it all.

Living a life for Christ is not easy. Many people enter this lifestyle thinking "once I give my life to God, everything is going to be better," and that's true. But it's important to remind you that the things that we once loved before we received Christ may be things that we still love and desire since God does not strip us of our desires or free will once we receive salvation. That means that we may still desire to be around people or in places that we once associated with before getting saved. The church mothers used to punk us into being saved and tried to scare the absolute hell out of us. And for those who grew up churched like I did; you know that I also mean this literally. Trust me, they told us all about living holy. "Don't do this, don't say that, don't wear this, please don't think that." But they certainly didn't show us how to live holy and enjoy Jesus! Now that *is* laughable. According to them, you weren't supposed to enjoy Jesus. You served Jesus. Our gifting wasn't fun or anything to be celebrated. Quite the contrary, our gift was for ministry, and ministry was serious business.

Once I received the Holy Ghost, I was both nervous and excited. I was nervous because although I was newly married, we were separated, and I didn't know how he was going to react to my newly found salvation. Honestly, I wasn't even sure that I wanted to return to the relationship, but I knew that since I was now saved, the expectation was to take the five hundred miles trip back home. "If you don't forgive him, God won't forgive you." I can still hear the voice of my pastor saying this.

I was excited because my life was in absolute shambles, and I believed that *my* salvation was going to somehow change *him*. For the sanctified wife sanctifies the unsanctified husband. That's what they always told me. "For the unbelieving husband is sanctified by the wife, and the unbelieving wife is sanctified by the husband" (1 Cor. 7:14). Boy, was I in for a rude awakening.

I desperately wanted to please God and please my new husband who had already showed himself unfaithful. I gave up *everything*—wearing pants, earrings, makeup, drinking, going to the movies, and all the other "damnable" things, and the list was exhausting! But I complied, even in spite of my husband's disapproval and his claim that my being saved was "a breach of contract." True, our lives had changed. I was no longer the young, hot trophy wife that his friends fawned over. I had become the frigid, matronly wife with a list of things that were not "becoming to holiness." Imagine the impact that this made on an already-dying marriage. The truth was that, even after I gave up all these things, I still had trouble living saved because I was never taught that I could enjoy Jesus and the new set of standards made my husband more upset and even more controlling.

I still become emotional as I think about it. I had already been a failure in "the world" so to also be a failure in Christ was deflating. Couldn't I do anything right? Not according to my pastor's wife who told me that I was a poor example of a Christian. That if I were a good example, then my husband would follow. But because I wasn't, it was no wonder that he could not live right. It was no wonder he chronically cheated. Yeah, no wonder.

For the first time in my life, I considered what things would be like if I weren't alive. I was twenty-three, married, and mother to a very young child when I gave my life to Christ. And the church mothers were dogmatic; you were cast down at the altar for even small infractions. Seldom did they give real life experiences or show weaknesses. Naturally, this led me to believe that I was the only one struggling. But thank God for his infallible word that provided comfort. Peter writes in Romans 7:21, "I have discovered this principle of life that when I want to do what is right, I inevitably do what is wrong every time" (NLT).

If Peter struggled and he was one of God's disciples, who walked alongside Jesus, then there was hope for me. Not only that, I began to understand that struggle is a natural part of this Christian walk because we constantly contend with our free will. One thing that I constantly remind myself of is that it is a duel to my death. Meaning, every day I fight to live a life for Christ because I love God. So I pray, "Lord, help me to love what you love and to hate what you hate." To do so, I must put on the "whole armor of God" and "hide the word in my heart so that I do not sin against God".

Ephesians 6:11–18 reads:

> Put on the whole armor of God that you may be able to stand against the schemes of the devil. For we do not wrestle against flesh and blood, but against the rulers, against the authorities, against the cosmic powers over this present

darkness, against the spiritual forces of evil in the heavenly places. Therefore take up the whole armor of God that you may be able to withstand in the evil day, and having done all, to stand firm. Stand therefore, having fastened on the belt of truth, and having put on the breastplate of righteousness, and, as shoes for your feet, having put on the readiness given by the gospel of peace. In all circumstances take up the shield of faith, with which you can extinguish all the flaming darts of the evil one; and take the helmet of salvation, and the sword of the Spirit, which is the word of God, praying at all times in the Spirit, with all prayer and supplication. To that end, keep alert with all perseverance, making supplication for all the saints (ESV).

Prayer

Prayer, in layman terms, is a conversation with God. Prayer used to be such a dirty word and the source of my *absolute* frustration. Every time there was an issue, the pastor would simply say, "Pray about it." It literally did not matter the magnitude of the problem, "Pray about it" was always the answer. Little did I know that prayer was, in fact, the answer to all things. One paragraph will not do this any justice, so I will talk more about it momentarily. So stay with me.

Fasting

Fasting, another dirty word. Now who in their right mind wants to go without food? And back in the day, we did absolute fasts. Everyone went on a fast, so don't even think about eating anything between 12:00 a.m. and 4:00 p.m. on Wednesdays because that was National Fast Day. And there was no such thing as a Daniel fast.

We had no water, no gum, not a Tic Tac breath mint—*Nothing*! It's funny to think about how we used to sneak a sip of water or set our clocks to 4:00 p.m. with great anticipation of eating all the things that we envisioned throughout the day. I remember salivating over the microwave at 3:55 p.m., watching as my lunch steamed to perfection. But even that simple pleasure caused me to be chastised by the "seasoned saints." "If you are thinking about food instead of Jesus, your entire fast was in vain" and "if you didn't pray while you fasted, you just went on a diet." Wait, what? So, all of my headaches, growling stomach, and dizziness was for nothing? Even more comical was the twenty-four-hour fast, which went from 12:00 a.m. to 12:00 a.m. I would go to bed extra early and set my alarm to wake up at the end of my fast just to eat dinner. Can you imagine being so determined to eat that you set an alarm to wake up at 12:00 a.m. to eat? My children and I still laugh about this story today.

Though I make jokes about fasting, fasting is good for the soul. And things that are good for the soul blesses all facets of our life. Fasting does not change God, fasting changes us. It's a misnomer in Christianity that fasting on behalf of other people or entities changes the situation. In reality, fasting provides discipline for the individual believer. When I fast, I am giving up food, something that the body needs for its survival. If I can deny myself of food for a safe period of time, then I can also deny myself of worldly pleasures that are toxic to my Christian life. It's not simply about going without food; it's spiritual core conditioning. For the believer, it is vital. Through core conditioning, we gain strength, patience, diligence, longsuffering, and the ability to respond differently to negative stimuli. So instead of "laying our Holy Ghost down for a minute," we are able to make a more intelligent, well-thought-out, and controlled decision.

We can now utilize practical techniques such as outcome thinking, which challenges us to think about the outcome or consequence of our actions prior to engaging in them. In doing so, we keep ourselves out of trouble.

For example:

If I slap Sister Sassy in the church parking lot, I will either end up in the back of a squad car or on the front page of the *Fresno Bee*. Headline reads: "*Local pastor's wife, psychotherapist, and founder of the HolyGhost HomeGirls assaults unsuspecting church member in the parking lot.*"

Since I do not want to embarrass myself, my family, my church, my God, lose my license, or go to jail, I should lick my emotional wounds and walk away. Yes, your pride may hurt a bit, but a one-year jail sentence and three years of felony probation would probably hurt more.

Reading the Bible

"Thy word have I hid in mine heart, that I
might not sin against thee" (Ps. 119:11).

I am the first to admit that this is easier said than done. I am not sure why most Christians find it difficult to read the Bible. But for me, it was because I didn't understand it, and some parts seemed to lack significance or relevance to my life. The most dreadful parts of the Bible for me was not the book of Revelation, which seemed to scare the novice Christian. It was the "begots" and the building of the temple #Snooze! Lord, forgive me, but my question was, why does anyone need to know this in modern times? And King James didn't make things any easier to digest. He didn't sound anything like my teachers in school nor any of my college professors. And since King James was the only version that we were "authorized" to read. I chose to omit reading the Bible from my daily regimen altogether.

I was elated when the complete Holy Bible came out on cassette tapes. I even overdrew my bank account so that I could purchase it. I remember sharing my excitement about listening to the Bible because the stories came to life, and I finally began to feel empowered, like a real Christian. Sadly, that feeling was short-lived because a sister in Christ chuckled sarcastically and informed me that "listening to the word of God was not the same as reading it…you need to sit and read the Word!" That was the last time that I listened to my cassette, and I didn't really bother to read the word either.

According to a 2012 study reported by *Christianity Today*, less than 20 percent of Christians read the Bible daily (Stetzer). And even more staggering, but not surprising, LifeWay Research points out that:

> Americans have a positive view of the Bible. And many say the Christian scriptures are filled with moral lessons for today. However, more than half of Americans have read little or none of the Bible. Less than a quarter of those who have ever read a Bible have a systematic plan for reading the Christian scriptures each day. And a third of Americans never pick it up on their own. Most Americans don't know first-hand the overall story of the Bible—because they rarely pick it up and the only time most Americans hear from the Bible is when someone else is reading it (Smietana).

Ladies, let's not pretend to be surprised. Instead, let us bow our heads and say, "Amen." What's that old phrase, if you can't say amen, say ouch? If we are honest and we are willing to take a self-assessment of our own Christian behaviors, most of us would probably realize that it's been a while, if ever, since we've read our Bible. Oh, that's right, I'm talking about me so that I don't have to talk about you.

I managed to survive nearly twenty years of my Christian life with little more than skimming the Bible. And, praying? Chile' Please! Though it may seem braggadocios, trust me, I'm not bragging; it's nothing to brag about. You notice I said, "Managed to survive." Doesn't surviving sound more like I escaped from something atrocious like a house fire, a debilitating ailment or like I was mauled by a bear, but I "managed to survive?"

But as I think about it, literally as I type, I did manage to survive something. I managed to escape and survive the clutches of the enemy despite my lack of diligence to the Christian fundamentals. Cue the organ because that alone is cause for a praise break! This speaks to the overwhelming mercy of our great God. He loves us even when we refuse to love and honor him by keeping his commandments.

Besides, when I wasn't reading my Bible or being committed to any of the Cristian coping skills such as fasting or prayer, I was anxious every day. I could hardly sleep, I was plagued by guilt, I was fearful that the rapture would take place, and ruminated over how I would be "left behind." I remember planning my response to the Antichrist and how thinking that I would be a martyr for Christ. I somehow believed that going through the tribulation and being beheaded would be easier than this "Christian walk."

I was constantly asking God for forgiveness because I knew that I was supposed to be more discipline. I wasn't necessarily doing anything wrong, but I wasn't doing anything right either.

Pardon me as I digress for a bit. But it makes sense to interject an important nugget here. I am known for dropping "notes, nuggets, and tidbits." So it's time to take more notes, sisters.

There are two types of sins: *sins of commission and sins of omission.*

Sins of Commission. These are intentional acts that we commit; a violation of God's mandates, the instructions that have been outlined in the Bible. Examples are lying, cheating, fornication, unnatural sexual acts, perversion, stealing, etc. Sins of commission are the sins that we, as Christians, tend be more conscious of. Likely because the Bible clearly defines these as sin and implores us to heed warning. Galatian 5:19–21 reads:

> The acts of the flesh are obvious: sexual immorality, impurity, and debauchery; idolatry and witchcraft; hatred, discord, jealousy, fits of rage, selfish ambition, dissensions, factions, and envy; drunkenness, orgies, and the like. I warn

you, as I did before, that those who live like this will not inherit the kingdom of God.

However, as many of us are learning as we mature and matriculate in Christianity, it is not enough for us to focus on not *committing* sin. In order to be successful in our Christian life, we must also be certain that we do not *omit* vital components that are necessary to maintain or properly care for our salvation. Just like our emotions, our lifestyle of Christianity must be properly cared for.

Sins of Omission. This refers to our failure to implement things that are consistent with Christian practices such as omitting prayer, fasting, reading the Bible, etc. Sins of omission are often ignored because the Bible did not specifically indicate that we must do these things to inherit the kingdom of God. Here are several scriptures that encourage us to use our Christian coping skills (prayer and fasting). If you haven't had the chance to read your Bible today, you're welcome!

> "Yet even now," declares the Lord, "return to me with all your heart, with fasting, with weeping, and with mourning." (Joel 2:12)

> But this kind does not go out except by prayer and fasting. (Matt. 17:21)

> Go, gather all the Jews to be found in Susa, and hold a fast on my behalf, and do not eat or drink for three days, night, or day. I and my young women will also fast as you do. Then I will go to the king, though it is against the law, and if I perish, I perish. (Esther 4:16)

> Is not this the fast that I choose: to loose the bonds of wickedness, to undo the straps of the yoke, to let the oppressed go free, and to break every yoke? (Isa. 58:6)

Cry aloud; do not hold back; lift up your voice like a trumpet; declare to my people their transgression, to the house of Jacob their sins. Yet they seek me daily and delight to know my ways, as if they were a nation that did righteousness and did not forsake the judgment of their God; they ask of me righteous judgments; they delight to draw near to God. 'Why have we fasted, and you see it not? Why have we humbled ourselves, and you take no knowledge of it?' Behold, in the day of your fast you seek your own pleasure and oppress all your workers. Behold, you fast only to quarrel and to fight and to hit with a wicked fist. Fasting like yours this day will not make your voice to be heard on high. Is such the fast that I choose, a day for a person to humble himself? Is it to bow down his head like a reed, and to spread sackcloth and ashes under him? Will you call this a fast, and a day acceptable to the Lord? (Isa. 58:1–14)

So he was there with the Lord forty days and forty nights. He neither ate bread nor drank water. And he wrote on the tablets the words of the covenant, the Ten Commandments. (Exod. 34:28)

As we have read, these scriptures do not condemn us to hell; rather, they challenge us to do these things and demonstrate a powerful move of God when we make the choice to utilize our Christian coping skills. That leads me to my next question: how do we live a sanctified life, which means to be set apart for the use of Christ, if we are not praying, fasting, reading our word, or going to church?

I read a very funny meme on Facebook. I don't know the source, but it is certainly worth the mention (see figure 1).

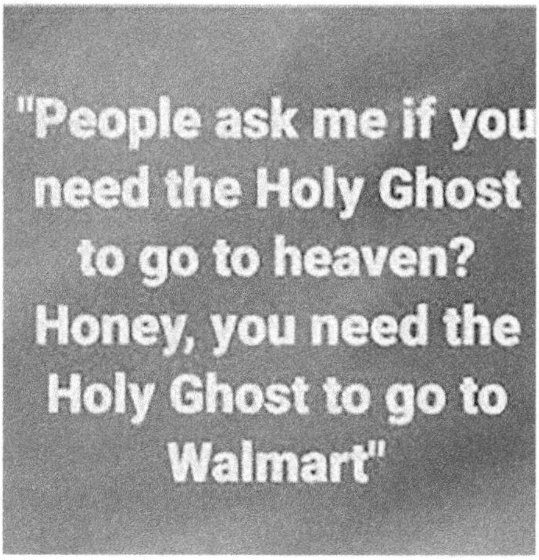

Fig. 1. Facebook Meme; source unknown

Our Christian coping skills help us to maintain the Holy Ghost, more commonly known as the Holy Spirit. The Bible tells us that having the Holy Ghost is the only way to inherit the kingdom of God. But please do not take my word for it! John 3:2–6 reads as follows:

> There was a man of the Pharisees, named Nicodemus, a ruler of the Jews: The same came to Jesus by night, and said unto him, Rabbi, we know that thou art a teacher come from God: for no man can do these miracles that thou doest, except God be with him. Jesus answered and said unto him, Verily, verily, I say unto thee, Except a man be born again, he cannot see the kingdom of God. Nicodemus saith unto him, How can a man be born when he is old? Can he enter the second time into his mother's womb, and be born? Jesus answered, Verily, verily, I say unto thee, Except a man be born of water and of the Spirit, he cannot enter into the kingdom of God. That which is born of the flesh is flesh; and that which is born of the Spirit is spirit.

Our coping skills should be used: (a) as an intervention to combat difficult life situations and (b) preventatively in order to create a lifestyle that does not invite or is resistant to spiritually hazardous situations.

Let's use a natural example to discuss the need for maintenance of a desired lifestyle.

Say we have battled alcoholism for ten years, but we successfully completed a treatment program and have been sober for a few months; it is also helpful, and some may even argue necessary, to attend Alcoholics Anonymous (AA), Celebrate Recovery (CR), or the like. Not only attend, but we must also practice the steps that are associated with these programs such as the twelve steps in the Big Book or, in the case of CR, read and practice the guidelines outlined in the Bible coupled with skills learned in group. Doing so keeps one disciplined and keenly aware of potential threats to our sobriety. Once we begin to deviate or fail to implement these steps or guidelines, the desire to return to alcohol returns or intensifies. For this reason, it is necessary to be proactive and take the necessary precautions to protect our sobriety or recovery.

As a young Christian, I knew exactly what I was supposed to do to maintain Christianity because the principles were drilled into me, and I was constantly reminded of my shortcomings. What I didn't know was how to apply these principles to my life. I lacked skill. In chapter 1, I told you that I was a psychotherapist and that I was licensed to treat mental health conditions. I also said due to lack of competence in some areas, I refer out when necessary. Well, this is an example of lack of competence. I had the Holy Ghost, so I had the license or authority to live a life that was pleasing to God. But due to lack of training in certain areas, I lacked competence. I had no idea how to be a young saved wife to an unsaved husband, while trying to also raise kids without half killing them. Don't you believe that a referral was in order? Yeah, me too. Here's another old adage: "Once you know better, you do better."

I believed that I loved the Lord and knew that I feared him. But the problem wasn't necessarily with my love for him; I had a skills problem. I didn't know it then, but I could not commit because:

1. I didn't really know God. I was serving God out of obligation and fear of hell, not because he was the lover of my soul and that I knew him to be the Lord of my life.
2. I hadn't been taught how to serve the Lord. I had a license, but I didn't have any keys.

Don't get me wrong; I'm not blaming anyone. I think my folks did the best that they could with the information that they had at the time. I saw my mother and father pray, fast, teach Sunday school, lead auxiliaries, and read the Bible. When my parents were committed to going to church, things were great. My daddy was a hardworking entrepreneur who owned a construction company. He was proud of his family, and he made sure that we had a beautiful home, one of the nicest in West Fresno. And my mother owned her own beauty shop. Dad took his family out to eat every Friday night and the other six days, Mom cooked a delicious home-cooked meal. The entire family sat together as we dined and shared the events of our day. Dad led the family in prayer as we "blessed our food" and his children, all five of us, would go around the table one by one and recite a Bible verse before we piled food onto our plates. We had regular family vacations, and life was good! It was during the times in our earlier years when my parents deviated from Christ, and we stopped going to church that life seemed unbearable. And unfortunately, because I was already greatly impacted by the abuse, it was difficult to recover and move on without professional help. In order to become proficient at any task, even reading the Bible, we must practice. My daughter, Essence, said that "practice doesn't make perfect, practice makes permanent." That is a quote that sticks. I must remind her to thank her college professor for that golden nugget!

Through my trials, I have learned so many valuable lessons about myself. As I spend time at the feet of Jesus, I realize that I am not as jacked up as I once believed. Okay, I am, but his perfect love covers a "multitude of faults." So today, I don't look like the hell that

I've been through. I have come to realize that I am a phenomenal woman who is great at many things. And today, I actually believe that. I will brag on the God in me later, but right now, I must point out a crucial flaw.

I have ADHD in the spirit, and I hate to read. I know you are asking how a self-proclaimed, lifelong student, and practitioner hates to read. Unless it's a juicy novel, preferably a romantic comedy, or something that I wrote, it likely does not hold my attention for very long (it's okay to laugh, I must admit that's a bit arrogant...but it's definitely true). In order to read and comprehend something that bores me, I typically need to do four things:

1. Read aloud. I often repeat the same sentence multiple times.
2. Sit in a quiet place without interruption, even if I have to threaten the kids to "shush or get slapped." Remember that slave mentality that I spoke about in chapter 1? Many things are still a part of my emotional fabric, and I am still unlearning these behaviors, so that the cycle of abuse stops with me.
3. Schedule enough time to thoroughly read the information without being rushed.
4. Take short breaks.

Since I am aware of these things about myself, I invest in audio books, and I set good boundaries. I thank God for the inventor of the Bible app and other apps that convert text to audio! Cue another praise break! Because I know that Jesus was looking out for me. He was like, "Let me help this po chile' out. Without this app, she may never read more than a verse or a few sentences at a time."

This brings me to another valuable *tidbit* for us all. *Ladies, know your limits, admit to your deficits, and stop trying to ignore your flaws.* We are not fooling anyone. Everyone can see that we lack in certain areas, and they are likely praying that we get ourselves some help so that *we* can get off of *their* nerves. So, it is imperative that we acknowledge our flaws and gain the skills necessary to be successful despite our limitations. As I continue to learn about myself through God's reflection of love for me, I realize that I am amazing. Sometimes, I just look at myself and the things that God has allowed me to overcome and I say, "Wow, God, you did that!"

Psalm 139:14 emphatically declares, "I am fearfully and wonderfully made." It goes further to say, "I know that full well." This lets me know that, as we celebrate the beauty that God has created in us, we are exalting him and his handiwork. Thus, I am no longer fearful of saying that I am a great friend; that I am compassionate, benevolent, loyal, (but I have boundaries). I am trustworthy, confidential, and I am an incredible, reflective, and empathetic listener. Basically, I am the best friend that you've always wanted. I can also say that I have learned to be a good mother, and I do my best to love, honor, and nurture my children. I do not abuse them or murder them with my words. I remind them that they are beautiful and smart, and I allow them to have an opinion and an opposing view.

I still have a bit of "crazy black mama syndrome" in me so I constantly fight the natural inclination to tell them that I will slap them into next year. I still have that annoying pitch in my voice at times when I get upset and yell like a mad woman, just like my mama did. But many of the generational curses have stopped with me because I am intentional about being better.

The beautiful, rich word of God reminds me of whose I am and that my children are a blessing that I have been trusted to nurture, groom, and raise in the admonition of the Lord. The fact that we were created with purpose in the very image of God, coupled with our flaws, simply adds to the beautiful complexity of our humanity.

I said all of this to say that reading the Word of God is crucial to the life of the believer the woman of faith. If you have trouble reading the Word of God because you are an auditory learner like me, consider an app and simply press play. After all, you can't hide the word in your heart, if you don't place it there first. And sisters, eventually, we want to thrive rather than merely survive.

Communion of the Saints

There is something therapeutic about being amongst friends. I love the way David scripted it in Proverbs 27:9, "A sweet friendship refreshes the soul." Have you ever had a long exhausting week, where everything seems to go wrong? Or a day when things are just off? Sometimes, we find ourselves in a predicament where we just need to be in the presence of others who "get us," who understands our Christian struggles, or at least doesn't count our struggles as foreign. That's how I feel about going to church and hanging with my Kingdom sisters, who I call my HolyGhost HomeGirls. They are my friends; my ride or dies in the faith. We are all trying to navigate through our Christian lives and when I am feeling low, I can depend on someone to say, "Keep going!" "You got this!" or "Girl, you betta' okay?" Or put the Word of God on it, "No weapon formed against you shall prosper," or "Better is he that is in you, than he that is in the world."

Sure, we can listen or read the word for ourselves, we can pat ourselves on the back, and positive self-talk is AH-mazing! But it just feels differently when our sisters remind us of the promises of God. Because, then, we know that we are not alone.

Here are a few passages that support the need to come together as a body of believers:

> And let us consider how to stir up one another to love and good works, not neglecting to meet together, as is the habit of some, but encouraging one another, and all the more as you see the Day drawing near. (Heb. 10:24–25)

> Praise the Lord! Praise God in his sanctuary; praise him in his mighty heavens! Praise him for his mighty deeds; praise him according to his excellent greatness! Praise him with trumpet sound; praise him with flute and harp! Praise him with tambourine and dance; praise him

with strings and pipe! Praise him with sounding cymbals; praise him with loud clashing cymbals! (Ps. 150:1–6)

Let the word of Christ dwell in you richly, teaching and admonishing one another in all wisdom, singing psalms and hymns and spiritual songs, with thankfulness in your hearts to God. (Col. 3:16)

I was glad when they said to me, "Let us go to the house of the Lord!" Our feet have been standing within your gates, O Jerusalem! Jerusalem—built as a city that is bound firmly together, to which the tribes go up, the tribes of the Lord, as was decreed for Israel, to give thanks to the name of the Lord. There thrones for judgment were set, the thrones of the house of David. (Ps. 122:1–9)

For where two or three are gathered in my name, there am I among them. (Matt. 18:20)

My Kingdom sisters, we are simply better together. Deuteronomy 32:30 says, "For one can chase a thousand but two can put ten thousand to flight."
Hallelujah!

Prayer and the Believer

I was being slightly facetious when I said that I have ADHD in the spirit. I said that because my prayers used to be all over the place, and they would bounce around like Tigger. This is still true today if I am not mindful of my propensity for distractibility. I prefer to pray using a list and a format that works for me. So, I guess you can say I have a pre-prayer before I pray. I first sit and list all the wonderful attributes of God literally, from A to Z. See table 2 below.

Table 2. Attributes of God Example

A	B	C	D
Amazing	Beautiful Savior	Custodian of my heart	Deliverer
Astounding	Bread of Life	Cross bearer	Defender

(Tidbit: I use a sharpie or dry erase marker to
write love notes to God or reminders about what
he has given me on my bathroom mirror.)

This is a technique that I thought of years ago when I was first learning to pray. I enjoy it immensely, and I continue to utilize it. There is something amazing about worshipping God. Talk about soul food! Telling God who he is, is a form of vertical worship. The act of asking for nothing, withholding nothing, simply telling God who he is to you! Next, I jot down a few things that I want to pray about, turn on my worship music, lock myself in a clean, confined space and begin to pray.

Most days, I can make it through the list of attributes. Other times, I get totally captivated by worshipping God that my soul is completely satisfied. I just say "amen" and begin my day. Some of you may notice that I said I lock myself in a "clean, confined space." That's because a messy room distracts me. When I walk into a messy space, my mind begins to wonder how it became messy to begin with, followed by thoughts of what I need to do in order to get it organized. If I don't have time to clean it, my anxiety peaks. Therefore, I pray in a clean room so that I focus on God and keeping this anger in check. If you stick around, I will share an outline that I use to help my sisters enhance their prayer lives.

Even in my daily life, I am hypervigilant and notice the minutest details. This makes me an awesome psychotherapist and intercessor, but it also throws me off track sometimes. That's because my mind grabs a thought and runs with it like a toddler with a stolen Twinkie.

Earlier in my marriage, Tobaise, who is my current husband and my "forever person" would become frustrated with me. The reason for that is that, given the situation, I may have trouble following a conversation. He would walk into a room while I was scrolling Facebook, watching TV, or eavesdropping on someone else's conversation and, without warning, he would begin talking. Immediately, my thoughts would be pulled in two different directions, and I would become a bit anxious.

Try to visualize this, I am fully enthralled in the latest fake news, and in walks, Butterscotch.

Oh, that's my nickname for Tobaise because he is fair-skinned and ultra-sweet. But here he came pulling me in, unsettled emotions and all. It's not enough to shake my head and to pretend to listen (I lack the ability to do this anyway), he was wanting the "honor of my eyes." But the problem is, I had something else competing for my attention. Even if I try to listen to him and tune the other thing out, I cannot. It exceeds my mental capacity. Therefore, I would become frustrated and nervous.

I will try to give you an idea about the dialogue that happens in my head during a situation like this.

"I really love Tobaise. He is caring and thoughtful and never attempts to shut me down. Sure, he is messy and *never* picks up his socks or anything else for that matter. Of course, he drives me nuts because his side of the room looks like a tornado hit it, and that tornado continued to grab his things and sling them around the entire house as well. But he is my forever person, and the good outweighs the bad. Right now, he wants me to listen to him and since he pays the bills and is kind to us, he deserves to be heard. If I don't stop what I am doing and listen to him, he will think that Facebook is more important than he is (although it *is* quite interesting). He will eventually become tired of being ignored and stop talking to me altogether. He will then begin to confide in others. And with my history of men cheating, I know this is often how infidelity begins. I'd better stop what I'm doing and listen to him. But If I do, he will continue to think that he can disrupt my quiet time whenever he wants and that will frustrate me. If left untreated, it will eventually infuriate me, and I cannot sustain another divorce ...oh boy, I'm practically screwed!"

Stop!

Ladies, do you see how I worked up an entire crazy woman dialogue in my head? I created an alternate scenario, one that was not presented. In psychology, we call this catastrophizing.

According to Psyche Central, catastrophizing is an irrational thought that leads us to believe that a situation is far worse than it actually is. Catastrophizing can generally take two different forms:

1. It can lead us to make a catastrophe out of a current situation.
2. It can lead us to make a catastrophe out of a future situation.

But this is what anxiety does. It creates an irrational narrative which often leads to an unwarranted irrational response. I had practically planned our divorce.

Instead of catastrophizing, I now ask him to give me a few moments to finish ear hustling, or I stop and pause my fake news so that I can give him the attention that he deserves and still maintain healthy boundaries in my life. Otherwise, I only hear a fragment of what he is saying, and we both become frustrated because my attention was partially tethered to Facebook, and I would swear that we never had any such conversation.

So, what does this have to do with prayer? Nothing, this was an example of me going off on an inattentive tangent.

But inadvertently, it has everything to do with my *unstructured* prayer habits! Despite the hype, prayer is not always some mystical earthshaking phenomena that pulls us into an impermeable trance. In fact, that rarely happens anymore, if ever; and it's *never* happened to me.

Prayer is not a trance or supernatural stupor; it is an intimate conversation with God. A conversation that takes on many forms, depending on our personality. Such as my need to write lists and begin prayer by reading with adjectives that I use to describe God. I discern that I may have lost a few of you with my theory about prayer. But I am here to tell you *my* truth and encourage you to consider the possibility that my theory has some validity.

Hindsight is 20/20, and I wish I would have understood and appreciated the value of prayer in my early Christian life. If I had, maybe I would not have omitted prayer from my life. The book of Joel says it best, "And it shall come to pass that everyone who calls on the name of the Lord shall be saved." I understand this to mean that our savior meets us at our place of need, regardless of our ability to conform to a template for prayer. Instead, we are invited to come to Jesus or speak to him in the best way that we know how, lists, distractibility, and all.

Being raised in church, I had many ideologies and false expectations about God and what constituted a relationship with him. This included many false perceptions of what prayer was supposed to look and sound like. We were not engaged in the act of prayer if we were not on our knees, with eyes closed, and fully engaged for at least an hour. Actually, it was said that we had not even touched heaven if tongues did not flow with fluency. My attempt to conform to this structure is one reason that I struggled with prayer in the past. I attempted to assimilate to church culture instead of having a conversation with my Heavenly Father. Recently, a prayer leader barked for everyone to close our eyes as she prayed. I looked away out of respect, but as an intercessor, God deals with me differently. He shows me things in the spirit as I pray and moves me to go and pray with others. (Tidbit: It is important that you follow the protocol of the church.)

I always had doubts about my love for Jesus, and I was not sure that I had ever really had the Holy Ghost living inside of me. We were always told, "The Holy Ghost would make you act right," "The Holy Ghost would make you live right," and "The Holy Ghost would make you do right when you want to do wrong."

So if I *truly* loved Jesus, then why wouldn't I keep his commandants? If I *truly* loved him, wouldn't being saved be easier for me? If I *truly* loved him, didn't that mean that I would not fall into cyclic sins of omission, and later ask for his forgiveness. Certainly, I could not possibly love God or have his spirit residing in me since this new life did not come naturally to me.

Truthfully, I missed my "old" unsaved friends because my church friends were boring, and we didn't talk about anything other than God. I privately cursed folks out in my head on a regular basis, and I desperately missed the pretty girl that I used to be prior to trading in my Guess jeans and K-Swiss for my new wardrobe of sackcloth and ash—I mean, jean skirts, and tennis shoes. If I loved God, why did I still desire to be attractive? Shouldn't these super-fluous, vain, desires have been swept away, left in the baptismal pool, and eradicated by my new commitment to Christ? Why were my prayers awkward, clumsy, and jumbled? Why did songs and lyrics come to my head instead of structured prayers as outlined in Matthew?

How could I tell anyone that prayer was monotonous, dry, and parched as a dusty beaten path? That the room didn't shake; that my tongues were more consistent with vain babble than my "spirit making intercession for me." Why couldn't I say that my new life was far from glorious and that I drifted closer to depression each day? I believed that I was doomed to hell, destined to fail and, for fear of ridicule, I could not say anything aloud.

The difficult thing was, I wanted to be a prayer warrior, and I seriously tried. I practiced shouting with exuberance, mimicking the staunch church mothers as they prayed. When they prayed, the room roared, and I felt something ignite in me. My spirit was quickened. Maybe it was the soulful hum, the vibrato of their anointed voices, the way their bodies swayed, or the way their hands became cymbals and their feet transformed into a mighty orchestra. Whatever it was, it wasn't happening for me when I prayed.

I mentioned earlier that I have always believed that I was different than others around me. Although I enjoyed and was empowered by the prayers of others, my prayers were different. In fact, they were so different that I did not recognize them as prayers. I didn't realize that God had been speaking to me my entire life and that he placed lyrics in me, lyrics that were intended to be given back to him. I didn't realize that the inexplicable energy in my body was gifting of my God coming alive in me, and I unknowingly had suppressed it for years.

Your Holy Spirit,
Something I can't quite describe.
Unable to articulate;
For what human utterance can capture a
presence so profoundly great?
What fragmented sentence doth my limited vocabulary transcribe?
As if I'm soaring;
Elated. Translated. Captivated
My soul flies, though my lying eyes deceive;
Raptured in glory, yet solid ground beneath my feet?
Alone with my savior
Just me, my redeemer, and I.
Melody in silence, beyond the noise;
Taking flight on heavenly chords.
Wind on my face,
His radiance kisses my skin;
Raptured in His presence,
Abiding in the Heavens
Still grasping for words,
though my lips find no relief;
Delightful! Splendid!
Utterly, completely, breathtaking!
Melancholy no more, mundane never again;
Eagles now my comrade, sparrows my kin.
…Inhale…
I breathe in the King of Glory.
Aromatic
Euphoric
Taking it all in;
As mist from the fount' glistens upon my skin.
Like honey, remnants of His presence remain;

Ah! What futile attempt to give a glimpse
of what cannot be explained
Your Holy Spirit;
Mortal words cannot describe
Inexplicable.
At a loss for words, silence finds me;
Through grateful lips, I simply whisper…
Come, taste, and see.

It took me nearly twenty years to figure out that this is prayer, too. Unorthodox, I'm sure, as I said I'm different than most. Although I still refer to myself as "different," artistic is a better description. When my dad called me a "silly child who would try anything once," he was not completely incorrect. I chose to reframe my thoughts by changing my perspective of being different. Now I look at "the child who would try anything once" as the part of me who loves a healthy challenge and the exhilaration of learning new things. Once I understood that there wasn't anything "wrong" with me and my failure to comprehend was based on my learning style, my confidence in my abilities began to grow.

Can we take a few moments to explore seven different learning styles? I assure you this is on topic. They are:

1. Visual (spatial): You prefer using pictures, images, and spatial understanding.
2. Aural (auditory-musical): You prefer using sound and music.
3. Verbal (linguistic): You prefer using words, both in speech and writing.
4. Physical (kinesthetic): You prefer using your body, hands, and sense of touch.
5. Logical (mathematical): You prefer using logic, reasoning, and systems.
6. Social (interpersonal): You prefer to learn in groups or with other people.
7. Solitary (intrapersonal): You prefer to work alone and use self-study.

Overview of Learning Styles

If we examine these learning styles, we will find that we primarily fit into one of these categories, although we may also fit into a combination of two or three. Leave it to me to have three separate categories that define me perfectly. Can you guess which categories I fit into?

If you said aural, verbal, and visual, you are correct!

No wonder I had difficulty with comprehension of the written word (Bible)! It's also no surprise that my prayers came alive with great animation when I recited them as poetry or spoke them aloud.

For too many years, I resisted my learning styles and shoved myself into templates instead. Imagine trying to squeeze into a pair of Spanx three sizes too small. Was that visual as painful for you as it was for me? I was attempting to force myself to use someone else's template for prayer. Every time I tried to pray in the manner that I was taught, I became frustrated. It did not work for me so consequently, I didn't pray. And because I did not pray, I was spiritually weak and emotionally destitute.

Poor choices and spiritual immaturity were leading me to a lifetime of destruction. At twenty-nine years old, my feet were weary from running and my heart was filled with holes. I was on a collision course headed for impact with my second divorce—this one more painful, destructive, and tumultuous than the first. I knew that something had to change.

I was pregnant with my third child and literally one self-deprecating thought away from being institutionalized. I was alone and hiding out in my three-thousand-square-foot home, confined to the only room that I could tolerate. My matted hair, my pillow, and the commode were my only companions. I lay on my bathroom floor for two weeks. I couldn't bear to eat, and I was too laden with pity to call for help.

I was close to death as my weak, shriveled, and desperately dehydrated body had nothing else to give. As I lay there wallowing in my own filth, a million miles from peace, I could not recall any words to pray. No template came to mind, and there was no hope in sight. The only thing that I could muster up was the fragmented verse of a song. And through chapped dehydrated lips, I whispered the words. "I can't find the words to pray. I'm a little down today. Can you help me? Can you hold me? I feel a million miles away, and I don't know what to say…" And right there, right in the middle of my confusion and despair, my savior met me. That moment changed my life, and my journey to healing began.

Everything that I once believed about prayer and God was now under investigation. This moment sparked new excitement for me, and a new love affair with the Father began. I had finally known him to be *my* savior.

From that day forward, I began to talk to God much differently. Rather than a litany list or a set of rules to abide by, I simply began talking to my Father. I mean literally, just like he was in the room. We had detailed, graphic conversations. The candor that I brought to him; at times, I would complain and cry while other times, I would sing. Like a child, I sulked, asked why, sobbed, and belted out inaudible screams. I danced and swayed, wrote, walked, and created. I cried some more while my very own lyrics I eloquently, poetically stated. At times, I sat in silence, with nothing at all to say. And my God held me through it all. I heard his gentle voice whisper, "Daughter, I would have it no other way."

As promised, here is the activity that I created to assist my sisters to enhance their prayer life.

The Power of Personal Prayer (Activity)

Ask, and it shall be given you; seek, and ye shall find; knock, and it shall be opened unto you: For every one that asketh receiveth; and he that seeketh findeth; and to him that knocketh it shall be opened. Or what man is there of you, whom if his son ask bread, will he give him a stone?

Or if he ask a fish, will he give him a serpent? If ye then, being evil, know how to give good gifts unto your children, how much more shall

your Father which is in heaven give good things
to them that ask him? (Matt. 7:7–11, KJV)

What are the vital components of a healthy interpersonal relationship? (Quickly jot down your thoughts and explore them with a
partner or a small group.)

a. _____
b. _____
c. _____
d. _____

Now considering the components of a healthy interpersonal
relationship *as indicated in question 1*, explore the cost-benefit anal-
ysis of nurturing a relationship using the components that you have
outlined. (Document and Discuss with your partner or group.)

_____
_____
_____
_____

How does a relationship with God differ from our human,
interpersonal relationships? (Document and Discuss with your partner or group.)

_____
_____
_____
_____

Next, being as honest as you can, identify which prayer scenario
best describes your current situation. Please be prepared to share out.

a. I have a scheduled prayer regimen, and I stick to it reli-
giously.
b. I intend to pray daily; however, I have not been able to
earnestly commit.

c. I say a prayer before bedtime.
d. I pray out of convenience, or if I need something.
e. My prayers mainly consist of blessing my meals.

Seven Steps to Effective Prayers (Activity)

If you are struggling with prayer and a template works for you, consider this outline.

1. Worship
2. Praise
3. Repentance
4. Pleading (for more of him)
5. Intercession (praying for others)
6. Declaration /Praying the Word
7. Reflection

In order to activate change, it is vital to have a viable plan. Let's discuss our plan of action to increase and enrich our prayer life.

Seven-Step Personal Prayer Action Plan

1. Set a _____! (time)
2. Create an _____ that is _____ to prayer. (atmosphere, conducive)
3. Accept that prayer requires _____ and _____! (practice, discipline)
4. Journal your _____. (progress)
5. Trust God with your _____, _____, and your _____! (emotions, madness, mess)
6. Ask for an _____ in your spiritual_____. (increase, appetite)
7. _____ with heaven by speaking _____ language. (cosign, kingdom)

Briefly discuss any insight that you have gained from the examination of prayer (communicating with God) and its connection to your overall relationship with him. Next, list the areas where you are strong versus the areas of prayer that need nurturing.

Strength	Needs Nurturing

As we conclude this chapter, I pray that we have been challenged to do a *soul assessment* by asking ourselves:

- How often do I pray?
- How often do I read/listen to my Bible?
- How often do I fast?
- How often do I attend church?
- How often am I in Bible class, learning and gleaning from my spiritual leader or pastor?
- When was the last time I repented?

Now, let's do a quick review.

1. A woman of faith knows that she belongs to God, and he alone can define her.
2. We glorify God when we celebrate the beauty that he has placed in us.
   - Celebrating his good works by adding value to others is not vanity, it's charity or love.
3. In order to live a solid life in Christ, we must utilize our *Christian coping skills.*
   - Prayer
   - Fasting

- Reading the Bible
- Communion of the saints (going to church and socialize with others of like mind)

4. Do not attempt to conceal your flaws; acknowledge them and find ways to work around them instead.

5. Do not attempt to squeeze into an ill-fitting template. Identify your learning style.

6. If templates work for you, find one that mirrors your personality, but make it your own.

7. Enjoy your time with God. There is no such thing as a wrong way to pray. He meets us at our place of need.

3

A GIRL AND HER GOD

Mean Girls

If I had a dime for every time someone called me mean, asked me why I always had an attitude, or asked me, "What's wrong?" I would be able to pay off my student loans, and I would no longer need to hide from Sallie Mae. People find it hard to believe today because I always appear happy, and my smile is always on display. But there was a time that I rarely smiled. First, it was that thing with my buck teeth, and the other times, I was offended or pretending to be. Thank God for an amazing therapist, the years that I spent finding deliverance at his feet, and a great orthodontist who helped me to find my smile again.

About ten years ago, as a county employee, the benefits department had provided me with erroneous information. As a result, approximately five to six thousand dollars had been taken out of my check over time. After several calls to rectify the issue and many conversations with supervisors, I continued to get the runaround. When I decided to go into the office and speak to management in person, I was met with adversity. Individuals I had spoken to in the past failed to recall conversations that had taken place over the past few weeks, and the supervisor on duty refused to acknowledge that I was waiting to see him.

One thing that did not escape me though is that I was a black woman in corporate America, and often, the only black woman in my department or office. So, I had learned to tone the "black girl passion" down. I mastered the art of walking slowly, speaking softly, forever smiling, and constantly reminding myself that my innocent hand gestures put white folk on guard.

When I was finally given the chance to meet with the supervisor, I sat quietly until I was invited to speak and, once given the opportunity, I calmly, although emotional, and fighting tears, explained what had transpired. Clearly, I was frustrated, as I would imagine anyone in my position would be. Management knew that someone had dropped the ball, yet no one wanted to be held accountable. Instead of saying, "Mrs. Ali, I apologize that someone gave you erroneous information that has caused an impact on your family. However, the Policies and Procedures read…" He decided to taint my character instead.

A bolded line in the meeting summary report stated, "We could see that she was visibly upset." As I reread this sentence, it struck me a different way each time. Despite my poised demeanor, I was still labeled as the angry black woman in the room. This was my perception and based on the follow up conversation with my own supervisor, my perception was spot on.

It's one thing to be angry, it's another thing entirely to be angry and black. Although this book is not about race, I cannot omit the fact that me being black often determines if, when, and how I choose to respond to a situation. Because I had three children to feed and an integrity as a good employee and Christian to uphold, I chose not to fight this battle. Instead, I added it to my evolving prayer list.

I made a decision that better served me and the goals that I had in life. In order to come to this conclusion, I used the technique of outcome thinking. Outcome thinking is when you consider all possible outcomes before responding to stimuli. Using the previous scenario, an example of outcome thinking would be:

"If I attempt to fight or sue the county alone, without resources, attorney, etc., I will likely end up causing more problems for myself. Although they gave me erroneous information, it was ultimately my responsibility to read the PPGs for myself. What is the likelihood of me getting my money back? Would pursuing this possibly cause tension with my supervisors or affect future promotions? Would I need to take off multiple days from work to go to court and lose more money? Nett, the best decision is to cut your losses."

I was tired of being labeled as mean, especially when I wasn't mean at all. But it had become a label that I couldn't manage to shake. I felt like a beat-up package labeled, "defective" and instead of "fragile" or "handle with care." I was branded "perishable," as if I was subject to "decay or had the tendency to rot" (Perishable).

I was nineteen years old when I married for the first time. Remember Jake? This dude seemed to bring out the absolute worst in me. If you'd asked anyone else, he was charismatic, with his happy-go-lucky demeanor, rich skin, and incredible gift of gab. In the beginning, it was great, but then again, we married after knowing one another for only three months. I loved him, there was no doubt. And we had fun together. Had I known him a bit better though, if I hadn't rushed things along, I would certainly have a different story to tell.

I ultimately married the first guy who loved me. Although I had casually dated in the past, this was my first real relationship, and it was nice to be cared for. He bought me flowers and took me on real dates. I mean as real as it could be in a small, rural town with nowhere exciting to go. He paid for things whenever he had money, and he had a *real* job. He was a military man, and that was intriguing. I could imagine myself traveling the world and staying on the military base.

When I brought him home to meet my family, everyone seemed to love this high strung, yet polished guy. He is what I refer to as gangsta' in recovery. Like when the hood and corporate America collide. It was the week before we married that things became a bit rough. The arguments escalated, and we could not seem to agree on anything. I told myself, "Ttoni, you don't want to do this. It's not too late, walk away, and tell him that you changed your mind. Yes, Mom and Dad already spent money on this wedding, but this does not feel right." Now, any other time, I would have listened to that voice in my head, but for whatever reason, I was actually not using logic. I loved him, but I did not want to marry him.

But I heard my dad's words resounding in my ear. As he told my soon-to-be husband, "My daughter, her mind changes like the wind. She might decide that she doesn't want to be married anymore." How could I say that he was right? I wanted to prove my dad wrong; I didn't want to be indecisive. I wanted him to see that I could commit to something and make it work. I ignored the gut feeling, my intuition that I was making a big mistake.

It didn't take long for things to go from bad to worse. The arguing increased in duration and frequency. If it was arguable, it was on our "to-do" list. One of the most memorable arguments within our first year together was over a game of Spades. Thinking back, I should have bailed then. He hated to lose, so what was supposed to be a fun-filled couple's date night ended up with me trying to barricade the bathroom door from the inside, before he broke it off of the hinges. He never hit me; he was too clever for that. He managed to leave the relationship unscathed with his good record intact, but I'm sure his conscious was not clear.

We fought every day. I screamed, belittled, cursed, and slapped while he barked, shoved, and punched holes in walls. As things became more severe, he would force me against walls or scoop my body high off the floor; and without warning, let me go, as my flailing body fell, like a ton of bricks to the floor.

Before him, I had never had so much as a parking ticket. And one night, I found myself half-dressed in the back of a squad car. We had relocated back to Fresno by then, and we attended church every Sunday, Wednesday, and Thursday. With his natural inclination to serve, he earned the spot of the pastor's unofficial armor-bearer. Of course, this annoyed me since he wasn't bearing any fruit at home, and I had no problem telling him every time it came to mind.

This particular evening, we argued the entire way to Sunday night service, and I was in no mood for charades. I got out of the car in my short skirt, the one that he bought and insisted that I wore despite the church rules of skirts below the knee. I was embarrassed and well past angry that he made so many demands on me. I was beyond the point in my life where I had to succumb to the demands of anyone. "The husband is the head of the house." This butchered scripture was the only one that he seemed to recall.

The ride home that night is one that I won't soon forget. I kept pleading, "Will you just shut up and drive? Please stop talking to me." The sound of his voice was making my skin crawl. My head was pounding, and big brother (anger) was checking for me big time. Even at home, his rant continued as I showered and put our two-year-old daughter down for the night. I had reached my limit when he had cornered me in the room. Hot breath and spittle spraying on my face, I attempted to duck underneath his arms that had formed a V around me. And when I couldn't, I pushed his face with the palm of my hand and jerked away. Before I could leave, he grabbed my half-naked underweight body and flung me across the room. My daughter woke up screaming as I landed on her bed. As he came closer to me, I picked up a cardboard Tigger that had fallen from the wall, hit him, and ran to call for help.

When the officers arrived, he was holding his slightly bleeding arm, and I was taken into custody. I can still hear the contrived compassion in his voice and that awkward look on his face. "Don't worry, Ttoni, I will bail you out."

"Train up a child in the way he should go: and when he is old, he will not depart from it" (Prov. 22:6). My parents did not send us to church; we went as a family. The Fields family had a strong presence at WOJCC. We rolled seven deep and had varying talents. My brothers were amazing soloists and together, they brought the laity to their feet. My parents were teachers, heads of auxiliaries, and diligent, faithful followers of others. For the most part, they practiced what they preached. I never heard my parents curse, not even in my earlier years when Dad struggled with alcoholism, or during those times when we were tossed back and forth to Grandma's house. But this beauty still had a beast growing inside of her. And the years of abuse that I encountered and witnessed had served as a training course for me. Violence was second nature.

Social Learning Theory

Social learning theory emphasizes learning through the observation of others. This also includes learning what happens as a result of our behaviors (the things that we do) whether the results are favorable or not. Once I began to study psychology, I became more cognizant that daddy was not trying to keep us from enjoying our friends. His choice to disallow us to attend sleepovers and parties was not about him being "mean;" it was him providing stability and protection as a father should. His all too frequent, uncompromising "Nos" kept us from situations that our juvenile minds had no knowledge of.

He and Mom taught us invaluable life skills. Such as the value of a dollar, how to manage five children, a business, a commitment to ministry, and an incredible work ethic. Inadvertently, my parents also taught me that when you are overly stressed, you isolate, argue, fight, or abuse alcohol. And my grandmother taught me that children should be beaten into submission whenever they make a mistake or can't catch on quickly enough. Although child abuse and physical domestic violence were a thing of our past, aggression always found a way to represent itself. Always.

No, they didn't sit us down, textbook in hand and instruct us how to be aggressive. This is a case where experience was the best teacher. One trait that I did not perpetuate, however, was the physical abuse of my children. It's painful to admit this, but given the appropriate stimuli, lack of skill, and poor self-discipline, the propensity to abuse a child is there. I don't have the savage rage nor desire for my children to hurt. I want to protect them. But I can certainly see how abuse happens in families. Especially if people are not intentional about keeping everyone safe. I wish I could explain the science behind my ability to abandon one maladaptive coping skill while embracing the others.

Many may not hold the same opinion as I do on this one, since abuse is abuse. But I'm grateful that I am intentional about protecting my children, and I am also empathetic in this area. I couldn't even bare to spank my children because I remember what a lashing feels like and the emotional damage that it caused me. It caused me to be angry, spiteful, and mistrusting of adults. Sure, all forms of abuse are heinous, but I don't think that I would be able to live with myself if I were abusive to children.

But to annihilate a man with my words or slap him if I disapproved of his response? *That* seemed somehow justifiable. I could deduce a man down to nothing more than pectorals and facial hair without a thought. And I didn't need to rehearse my lines. I knew very well how to cut him down to his core. As complicated as it may seem, I viewed men as both the hero and the villain.

Is this a case of my sin being less significant than someone else's? Perhaps. But again, this is my truth, my own personal bias, and you'd better believe that we all have them.

Had my history of abuse and exposure to domestic violence caused me to be a degenerate when it came to romantic relationships? I would say so, since I couldn't seem to keep any man happy. They were infatuated with the exterior, but they were ultimately dissatisfied with the quality of the product.

The Princess Within

When it comes to love stories, Disney is the best. Cinderella and Prince Charming rode off into the sunset in a magical carriage to rule a kingdom, after her humility, grace, and captivating beauty gave provision for love to find her. Snow White, despite the loss of her mother and an attack on her life, Prince Ferdinand showed up to save the day and whisked her away. Sleeping Beauty won the heart of Prince Phillip, and they lived happily ever after.

The fact that these were only fairy tales did not stop this girl from the wrong side of the tracks from dreaming. My head always seemed to be in the clouds. I dreamt of traveling the world, seeing new things, learning new exotic languages, and marrying a millionaire who would get my teeth straightened and my nose "fixed." I was looking for a hopeless romantic who would shower me with lavish gifts, throw surprise parties, and unveil a '74 convertible Mercedes tied in a red bow while my friends toasted and watched in admiration. I giggle as I think about my childhood list of trivial desires.

My dad provided a very comfortable home and lifestyle for us, but I still dreamed of living in a mansion in the bluffs or ruling some enchanted kingdom.

After my second marriage came to a crashing halt, with me on the underside of his white BMW, I had begun to lose all hopes of a fairy tale ending. It wasn't quite the Mercedes that I dreamt of nor the series of events that I had imagined. But ironically, I did end up with the luxury car. I also ended up with an exacerbated sense of hopelessness, desperation and because this was now failed marriage number two, I was utterly humiliated.

What had I done to deserve this life? Why was I the one to suffer chronic extramarital affairs, the verbal attacks, controlling behaviors, and the ridicule from my husbands' lovers? I was far from perfect, but by societal norms, I was a good citizen. I didn't set out to hurt others. I was not a person who took pleasure in seeing others suffer. In fact, most of my issues stemmed from my compassion for others. Even when others hurt me, seemingly intentionally, I didn't want to reciprocate. I tried to reason with them. Tried to convince them to be kind to me so that I could love them in return. But that never seemed to work in my favor. This rejection left me in a state of desperation and often, overly reactive to stimuli. I knew that my life was in shambles, and the world around me was coming down like the walls of Jericho.

I cried myself to sleep most nights, hoping that I would not wake up. And when sleep escaped me, I thought deeply about who would care for my kids and how happy or saddened they would be. During those times. I could almost feel my heart breaking for my children because I knew they needed their mother. I also knew that no one could ever love them like I did. If only I could get my emotions together. My emotions were driving ninety miles per hour toward the edge of a cliff.

As I sat in that desolate parking lot like I had many times before, crying, alone, and in emotional and physical pain, I knew something had to change. I did not need another quick fix, nor did I need temporary relief from pain that would only last for a month. I needed a lasting change.

As fury grew in my belly, I had finally come to a place of reckoning. I would not allow any man to treat my babies the way that men had treated me. It was time for the cycle of violence to end. I was finally abandoning abuse, for good this time.

The Heart of the Father

"She brought an alabaster jar of perfume. As she stood behind Him at His feet weeping, she began to wet His feet with her tears and wipe them with her hair. Then she kissed His feet and anointed them with the perfume" (Matt. 26:37–38).

Karen Clark Sheard penned the lyrics, "The sweetest place in the whole wide world is in the will of God." These words have never held more meaning than at this time when I found myself in a broken, desolate, and desperate place.

There I laid, at the feet of my Father suffocating in self-pity and ratting out all wrongdoers. Hour after hour, day after day, I spoke my peace, unpacked the pains that I could no longer bear. Names, dates, I had receipts for all accounts. I had listed the infractions for every misdeed. I cried until my tears were no more, leaving nothing but vacant sobs. I could feel the warmth of his spirit, as I found my place safe under the shadow of his mighty wing. What a "wonderful counsellor" indeed (Isa. 9:6). Isn't that just like the Father to allow us to cast all our cares on him, for he cares for us? (1 Pet. 5:7). He heard my cries and dried my tears. He held me close and silenced my fears. No wonder we call him "the Prince of Peace."

After months of lying at his feet and saying all that needed to be said, I thought the conversation had ceased. That's when Jesus whispered to my spirit, "Daughter, now allow me to speak." It was then that the Lord began to show me his will for my life. Gently, he began to unveil things that I had somehow missed before or perhaps subconsciously evaded. He graciously began to uncover mistakes that I had made during the times that he said "no" or "Nett, not

DR. ANTIONETTE D. BROOKINS, LMFT PH.D IN CHRISTIAN PSYCHOLOGY

yet." Although it did not feel punitive, I continued to resist. "But, Father, look at what he did, fix *him* God, make *him* treat *me* better. Lord, please save him." But every time I pointed fingers at him, God showed me myself instead.

His illuminating grace became a reflection of my life as he played back the tape and showed the film. Jesus and I began watching the cinema of my life. Together, we explored his will, the choices I had made, the ways in which he was steering me in a different direction, and how, in my spirit of defiance, I chose the path of regret. The times that I drove recklessly on the highway of life and swam in unchartered waters with no lifeguard or safety raft in sight.

He reminded me of his words to me, the ones he spoke when I was a child. I began to see that he was always there, even when I could not see or feel him. I was overcome with grief, as shame and regret began to overtake me. But Instead of condemnation, he held me instead. Like a warm embrace, I could feel the heart of my Father.

Abba, the Greek word for "Father" and *Rabboni* literally being translated as "master" or "teacher" had begun to take on a new meaning. Jesus had now become my teacher and I began to pursue his instruction. "As the deer pants for streams of water, so my soul pants for you, my God" (Ps. 42:1).

> O God, thou art my God; early will I seek thee: my soul thirsteth for thee, my flesh longeth for thee in a dry and thirsty land, where no water is; To see thy power and thy glory, so as I have seen thee in the sanctuary. Because thy loving kindness is better than life, my lips shall praise thee. Thus will I bless thee while I live: I will lift up my hands in thy name. My soul shall be satisfied as with marrow and fatness; and my mouth shall praise thee with joyful lips: When I remember thee upon my bed and meditate on thee in the night watches. Because thou hast been my help, therefore in the shadow of thy wings will I rejoice. My soul followeth hard after thee: thy

right hand upholdeth me. But those that seek my soul, to destroy it, shall go into the lower parts of the earth. They shall fall by the sword: they shall be a portion for foxes. But the king shall rejoice in God; every one that sweareth by him shall glory: but the mouth of them that speak lies shall be stopped. (Ps. 63)

Every morning, I woke up with Jesus on my mind, and I found pleasure in laying prostrate before him. His words remained with me throughout the day and wandered into my dreams. He was showing me myself in a way that I had not seen before. There she was in all her beauty, an exquisite woman adorned in a pearly white gown. A silver crown nestled in her magnificent coils, satin gloves that graced her delicate arms, a train that flowed from the altar to the door, and her presence shone like the breaking of day. Although her face resembled my own, like Sarai, I chuckled at the very notion. I said secretly, as if my thoughts fell upon deaf ears, "I would never wear that. I am a very simple girl" and Jesus responded in the silence, "You dreamt of these things, although you never felt worthy. Daughter, you were created in my own image, beautifully and wonderfully."

These words lingered with me like a web that catches you off guard in the breeze. God said it so it must be true, right? I was taught to never question God, but it seemed fitting to do so. And thus, I continued to converse.

Me: "Lord, why is this so far from my own reality? I have a string of failed marriages and a lifetime of pain."

Lord: "From the men you chose and the decisions that you made, that was never what I planned for you. But you never asked."

True, I managed to keep God confined to the Bible that I rarely opened. But things were different now, I began to pray for his heart and his emotions. Every morning before sunrise, I continued to meet with him; faithfully, he was always there, and I was totally captivated by his presence.

Each day I laid broken before him and He spoke words that brought comfort, healing, and joy. He awakened a piece of me that had been dormant. This began my lifelong love affair with my father. My only desire was to render unto him the things that he had given to me—the abundance of my life, my whole heart, and, finally, my soul.

He offered me my birthright and a place to rest at his feet none of which men or the world could offer me. And now I had a new name—Princess Redeemed—for my Father is the King of kings. Once again, like a stream, the tears began to flow; only this time, they were tears of joy instead.

The Power of the Holy Spirit

Now that the scales had fallen from my eyes and I had become cognizant of who and whose I was, it was time to stop living beneath my privilege. I had begun to invest more time to cultivate my mind, cherish my body, and nurture my soul. My "spirit man" was under construction and for the first time in a long while, I was beginning to love the renovated version of myself. The broken and disenchanted girl who once glared back at me from the mirror now donned a brilliant smile, and it was no longer contrived.

Some find this hard to believe because I had mastered the art of illusion. But my disheveled life had nearly pushed me to a point of a complete nervous breakdown. Unless you were in my inner circle, or you happened to catch me on an off day when I could no longer contain my erupting emotions, most believed that all was well.

I was gainfully employed and had somehow managed to obtain a bachelor's degree in psychology and was in hot pursuit of a master's degree in marriage and family counseling. Marriage and family therapist seem oxymoronic, doesn't it? Perhaps somewhat hypocritical? A former pastor literally laughed in my face when I told him that I was pursuing this degree. With his cynical tone and mocking words, "What could you possibly tell anyone about marriage with your history?" Though the words stung like an unsuspecting pop, this was irony at its best and the favor of the Lord indeed. The Lord was allowing all of my failures and misdeeds to pave the way for the healing and the instruction of others. As my now husband, Sr. Pastor Tobaise Brookins, often reminds the congregants, "Never waste pain." My life had landed me in the starring role of an amazing testimony about God's redemptive power. And I am not ashamed to tell it!

Today, still closely connected to my teammates from my master's program, we celebrate God for the miracles that he performed in my life. We remain astonished by my determination, the ability to maintain a near perfect GPA, care for my children, and attend early morning prayer each day, especially given the hell that I endured during that time. I spared few details from my teammates because we were all women of faith, and their prayers and support were needed to get us all through these fast-paced courses and my catastrophic life.

From showing up to class with the back window in my car bust out for the third time, sifting through threatening texts messages from my ex and his family to my six months stay in a battered women's shelter, there were times when I was stretched to the max. But I persevered. If it weren't for statistics, my nemesis, I would have graced the stage with a different colored cord and a perfect 4.0. I was disappointed, but all A's and one C throughout my academic career wasn't exactly a failure.

The laughs that me and my teammates turned sisters have today about these accounts and how the devil thought he had me, but the Lord "worked it out for my good" and his own glory! That's the power of prayer and the Holy Spirit!

> "And we know that in all things God works
> for the good of those who love him, who have been
> called according to his purpose" (Rom. 8:28).

And if I may borrow a passage from my Bible *BFF* Joseph, my homeboy in the faith, Genesis 50:20 reads, "But as for you, you meant evil against me; but God meant it for good, in order to bring it about as it is this day, to save many people alive."

Even though times were hard, and there were many obstacles to overcome, I knew that I wanted more for my life and that purpose was in me. I knew that I wanted to live a fulfilled life in Christ, be successful, and help others in need. I also knew that I could not do anything without Christ.

For this reason, there were times that I barricaded myself inside my bedroom in order to submit assignments while my ex-husband mocked me from the opposite side of the door. "What kind of Christian are you? How are you going to teach anyone about anger when you are always angry yourself? You are a joke, even your pastor said that you are supposed to be submitting to me, you ain't no wife. Now come out here and give me some."

I had taken anger management courses two times before, and I walked away both times just as furious as the day that I began. But now, there was something different about me, someone was now operating through me. I allowed Jesus Christ to take control of my life, and I couldn't have been more thrilled. I was captivated, but there were no chains, no fetters, and no bondage. Now the overwhelming mercy and love of the custodian of my heart and the resurrector of my mind washed over me like a tsunami. And I was ready to show the world that the chapter of my life titled "Abuse" had come to an end.

This new chapter was a complete paradigm shift. Even my therapist was surprised by my ability to effectively manage emotions and my ability to resist being reactive to negative stimuli. She remarked at the end of one session, "You and Jesus make a good team." My smile was making regular appearances, and I gained a radiance that I had not possessed before. This was based on my choice to allow Jesus to be my savior and my Lord. The one who rescues, governs, and provides purpose and direction for my life.

"Jesus is the way the truth and the life" (John 14:6). And it was time to allow him to lead.

If it weren't for the strength of the Holy Spirit that had quickened in me, I am certain that I would have completely lost my mind and my composure during the final months of my marriage. But there was a stillness in me that had begun to provide peace that surpassed my ability to comprehend. "And the peace of God, which passeth all understanding, shall keep your hearts and minds through Christ Jesus" (Phil. 4:7).

I finally understood what the church mothers meant when they said, "He'll keep you if you want to be kept." And I also add, "He'll keep us even if we don't want to be kept." For I am a witness that the Holy Spirit will bypass our current state of mind, step into our future thoughts, and begin to operate on our behalf.

Isn't our God amazing? "Great is our Lord and abundant in strength; His understanding is infinite" (Ps. 147:5). Who wouldn't serve a God like this?

I will close this section with this final verse. "But you will receive power when the Holy Spirit comes on you; and you will be my witnesses in Jerusalem, and in all Judea and Samaria, and to the ends of the earth" (Acts 1:8).

4

BEAUTY AND THE BEAST

Beauty and Her Boundaries

"I don't do abuse anymore. I don't give it, and I don't take it."
This has become my personal mantra for my life. In fact, if I had a
soundtrack for my life, the intro would be Grandmaster Flash's "The
Message." "Don't push me 'cause I'm close to the edge; I'm trying
not to lose my head." Okay, sisters, I know it's not a good ole gospel
hymn, as one would suppose. But it's the truth!

Having nearly twenty years in recovery from the ailments of
life, I am not nearly as reactive or volatile as I once was. In fact,
my new lifestyle of intentional living keeps bad behaviors, dangerous
maladaptive thoughts, and my inner beast at bay. That's because I
have committed to keeping negativity and toxicity out of my life.
That includes people, places, and things.

Why? Because as children of God and daughters of the King,
our Father has granted us "beauty for ashes." "To appoint unto them
that mourn in Zion, to give unto them beauty for ashes, the oil of joy
for mourning, the garment of praise for the spirit of heaviness; that
they might be called trees of righteousness, the planting of the LORD,
that he might be glorified" (Isa. 61:3).

Sisters, I have mourned and sown enough tears for a lifetime, big brother has derailed enough relationships, and my inner beast— the despicable, volatile, hypersensitive, hypervigilant part that dwells within us all—has demolished enough rooms, thrown enough tantrums, pitched enough fits, and has literally brought my life to a screeching halt. Life has taught me enough about myself to know that my beast must remain in permanent hibernation, and I must walk circumspectly as not to rattle the cage. This is why the need for healthy boundaries is so critical in my life. Ladies, boundaries are a beautiful thing. They afford us the opportunity to maintain a life that is pleasing to God and enjoyable for us and those who love us.

> For ye were sometimes darkness, but now are ye light in the Lord: walk as children of light: (For the fruit of the Spirit is in all goodness and righteousness and truth) Proving what is acceptable unto the Lord. And have no fellowship with the unfruitful works of darkness, but rather reprove them. For it is a shame even to speak of those things which are done of them in secret. But all things that are reproved are made manifest by the light: for whatsoever doth make manifest is light. Wherefore he saith, Awake thou that sleepest, and arise from the dead, and Christ shall give thee light. See then that ye walk circumspectly, not as fools, but as wise, Redeeming the time, because the days are evil. Wherefore be ye not unwise, but understanding what the will of the Lord is. (Eph. 5:8–17)

I will quote myself and say, "Boundaries are a girl's best friend." As I mentioned earlier, this was a lesson sown in tears and reaped in joy (Ps. 126:5). For years, I allowed myself to be trampled upon. I put everyone else first and left myself with nothing more than scraps that were not enough to sustain me. Codependence and my unhealthy desire to make others happy were the very things that led to my own misery. The more misery I experienced, the angrier I became, and my anger was consuming me.

Like a cancerous cell, it was depleting every part of me. Soon, the only thing that people could see was the anger. No more joy, no more peace; like the woman at the well or the woman with the issue of blood, people had forgotten my name. I was known by my ailments instead; my deficits were the only thing that defined me. "Who, the mean one?" That was my name.

When I am working with clients, one of the things that I assure them is that I have no intention to strip anything away from them. Their ailments, deficits, and/or issues were all theirs to keep if they desired. Sisters, we only get one life, and it is ultimately ours to manage. Incidentally, we are the ones who determine who and what we allow to infiltrate our space, our emotions, and our lives.

As a psychotherapist, I choose to approach therapy this way mainly because of my own experiences with intrusive people. Before I had the capacity to make the necessary changes in my own life, I had no interest in the opinion of others. I didn't ask anyone what they thought, and when they interjected their "concern," it was met with adversity and, ultimately, avoidance.

For this reason, I allow others to be the captain of their lives. And I have a no judgment policy, because "it is what it is." It's my job as a therapist to help others to navigate their issues while upholding the Hippocratic Oath "to do no harm." I do, however, present the idea of change and begin to plant a seed that leads them to consider a quest for joy, fulfillment, and purpose in the process.

I don't want to be the reason someone makes a choice.

As an alternative to instructing others about what they should do, I offer clients my professional perspective. My role is to be a mirror that shows others themselves as I gradually and gently point out the consequences of the choices that they have made. Being a mirror allows them to see what others likely see when they see them. This mirror is not the ones with the harsh UV lights similar to the ones in the dressing room during swimsuit season. Rather, these mirrors use gentler, more natural light that highlights our assets while bringing awareness to areas that need attention. I provide a nonbiased, objective perspective as we explore alternative ways to handle any given situation.

At times, clients make the choice to remain in abusive relationships or continue to behave in a manner that is toxic to their well-being and hazardous to their emotional and spiritual health. In that case, we discuss safety planning, and de-escalation techniques, while we continue to work on self-esteem, self-worth, ways to foster healthy friendships, positive ego-strength and of course, exploration of resources. These are all necessary for people to feel confident enough to walk away from abuse or things that do not serve them.

But in order to properly gauge where someone is, I begin by asking one key question. "How is 'that' working for you?" What I am essentially asking is, considering the situation that brings you to treatment, or the issues that you were brave enough to share, how is this impacting your life and your ultimate desire for peace?

Before we as the onlookers say, "Obviously, it's not working, that's why they came to therapy!" Sisters, that's not necessarily true, some of us have no idea what the presenting issues are. We may be cognizant of the fact that we worry often, that everyone and everything works a nerve, that we feel sad most of the time, that our weight is fluctuating, that our edges are sparse, nearly nonexistent, and that our thoughts keep us awake at night, but we may not know why.

We may not understand that the very things that we hold dear or our bad behaviors or attitude is actually the cause of our calamity. Therefore, it is possible to deflect our issues and pain to an outside source, hold the belief that our misery is someone else's fault, or have absolutely no idea why we are sitting on our therapist's couch. It is true that others may contribute to our discontentment, but a pivotal question is, how they gain access or why do they continue to have influence over our peace.

Another important factor is, many of us are ignorant to the fact that someone or something is invading our "will not tolerate." We will discuss our will not tolerate in just a bit. Because of this, we remain in conditions with the belief that we have a higher tolerance for negativity, when in fact, our emotions and our bodies lack the ability to manage the stress.

To put things into perspective and highlight the need for boundaries in our life, here is a list of psychopathologies, common mental health symptoms.

- Lack of sleep
- Loss of joy
- Irritability
- Aggressiveness
- Apathy
- Lack of empathy
- Fatigue
- Isolation
- Decrease in activities
- Unexplained aches
- Feeling helpless
- Feeling hopeless
- Smoking
- Relationship problems
- Drinking
- Drug use
- Other risky behaviors
- Confusion
- Forgetfulness
- Ruminating or intrusive thoughts
- Hearing voices
- Having delusions
- Thoughts to harm self or others
- Inability to do normal tasks, i.e., care for kids go to work/school

Given the impact of these symptoms, there may ultimately be an inability to function in any given role at our full potential.

By God's design, our emotions and our bodies communicate with us. Remember our anger cues? Similarly, these are some ways that our emotions and bodies are telling us that we cannot tolerate the strain of our situation. Sisters, before we begin to panic and call upon the all-knowing Google for a diagnosis or reach for the latest self-help manual, it is important to understand that this list is by no means intended to serve as a mental health assessment. Rather this is to bring awareness about how stress can affect us, as well as how the lack of boundaries essentially subtracts from us.

That being said, if you find that you have highlighted more than a few of these listed items, I urge you to consider a lifestyle change. That begins with a follow-up with your primary care physician to rule out any medical conditions. Next, make an appointment to speak with a mental health professional. Collectively, these professionals can assist you in finding a greater quality of life, as well as a balance that adds value to your life rather than subtracts from your purpose.

Boundary violations among family and friends are not uncommon. In reality, these boundary violations occur more often with people who we are familiar and comfortable with. Let's explore this further. We will begin with defining two important terms: *boundary* and *violation*.

Boundary: "By definition, a boundary is anything that marks a limit. Psychological limits define personal dignity. When we say, 'You just crossed a line,' we are speaking about a psychological limit that marks the distinction between behavior that does not cause emotional harm and behavior that causes emotional harm" (Richmond).

I personally like to think of boundaries as a fence that protects our emotions and overall well-being. This fence keeps things intact such as peace, joy, harmony, sanity, and good health while denying access to other things such as negativity, fatigue, and toxicity. One thing that we may not consider, as it relates to our personal boundaries, is that our boundaries are not only for our protection, they are also for the protection of others.

As we continue with the concept of a fence, let's now imagine that there is an aggressive dog or beast on the inside of the fence. As long as the beast is contained, no harm can be done to passersby. Since the beast is inside the confines of its habitat, he or she is enjoying life and has no reason to attack. It's not until the boundary is violated and there is a threat of an intruder that both parties are in potential danger. The safety of both parties is at stake, the intruder who may be mauled, and the beast who may sustain offensive injuries as the intruder fights off the attack.

This leads us to our next definition.

Violation: According to the Oxford Thesaurus, a violation can also be described as a "breach, infringement, infraction, transgression, nonobservance, lack of compliance with, disobeying, disobedience, defiance, defying, flouting, flying in the face of, and rebelling against."

Nugget: *Boundaries are only as effective as the one upholding them. What good is setting a personal boundary if we ourselves violate them?*

Psychologically speaking, what are some benefits of setting boundaries? Please take a moment to ponder this question and document the response.

If we refer to the list of mental health symptoms, we will begin to see the need for setting boundaries in our life. If there are only one or two symptoms, congratulations! Things are going well, and you are managing to keep stress at bay. However, if you have an exhaustive list of psychopathologies, life becomes too difficult to manage without professional help because many symptoms can be insidious in nature as they gradually diminish your quality of life.

It's time to revisit the "will not tolerate." If we have said in the past that we could tolerate something and we are experiencing psychopathology, it's quite likely that we are either in denial or we are unaware.

In a previous marriage, I found myself struggling with nearly all the listed symptoms. My ex would often point out that I was "always irritated and overwhelmed," and although I despised him for saying it, it was true. In retrospect, I remember my chronic complaints of being irritated. Everything bothered me, I was seldom happy, and my nerves were always on edge. I cried on a near daily basis, and I was constantly looking for a reason to "fly off the handle."

Truthfully, I did not need another reason because he had given me plenty. With every new or recurring infraction, more and more good qualities were being subtracted from me. Although I knew things were bad, I had not come to the realization that I could not tolerate the treatment. I thought to tolerate something meant that you could remain in the situation. In reality, tolerance refers to one's ability to "endure continued subjection to something, especially a drug, transplant, antigen, or environmental conditions, without adverse reaction" (*Merriam-Webster*).

She probably does not realize this, but his mother, my former mother-in-law, is the person who planted the seed, which led to me walking away from my abuser for good.

Being a closet narcissist, he believed he was being helpful when he suggested that I call to consult with his mother. His desire was not to help me to recover; instead, it was a ploy for me to remain in a place of complacency and continue to groom my invalid self. His intent was to normalize his abusive, male chauvinistic traits by creating a bond through commonality with his mother who had "endured for years." He labeled me bipolar and attempted to pacify me with "psych meds." He told me, "Just call my mother…you guys should talk." In dire straits, I spoke to her with the hope of finding some resolve, disclosing all that had transpired during the span of our brief marriage. Instead of resolve, I found courage instead.

Her words still resound in my ear. "Well, you have to know how much you can tolerate." These were her words before she began to share things that she had "tolerated" in her own marriage, things I will not disclose for that is not my story to share. I remember hanging up the phone in disgust and making a vow to never allow my golden years to be tarnished by tolerating things that were contrary to my purpose.

Now being a stronger woman of conviction and faith, I understand what my Heavenly Father was trying to convey all along: "This is not what I planned for you, and I cannot allow you to remain living like a sow in squalor." But change had to be my choice. So instead of God fixing my ex, as I desperately prayed, he allowed me to be uncomfortable enough, hit my head enough, be confined enough, and suffer in jail long enough until I made the decision that enough was enough and to let go of the things that God had declared unclean. Like the prodigal child, it was time to return home. It was time to trust my Father in every area of my life, especially the area that I seemed to need him the most, my love life.

Establishing and maintaining healthy boundaries in a relationship adds stamina, joy, and longevity to the relationship. Likewise, the lack thereof creates conflict, resentment, and ultimately leads to the destruction of the relationship. A previous study indicated that being mistreated by one's romantic partner evokes anger, and that anger can motivate a reciprocation of the mistreatment, eventually resulting in a cycle of destructive behavior and rage (Liu et al.). See the cycle below (figure 2).

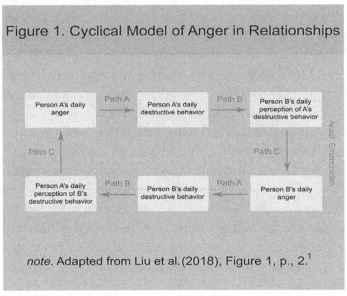

Figure 1. Cyclical Model of Anger in Relationships

note. Adapted from Liu et al. (2018), Figure 1, p., 2.[1]

Fig. 2. Cycle of Anger from: Emamzadeh, Arash. "The Cycle of Anger in Relationships." *Psychology Today*, 15 Jan 2019.

Here, Emamzadeh summarizes the cycle. As indicated by Path A (Fig. 2, top left section), feelings of anger sometimes trigger destructive behaviors—critical, cold, and selfish behaviors. These behaviors differ from respectful and constructive criticism, which focuses on the issue and does not attack the individual. In contrast, destructive behaviors are experienced as disrespectful, hostile, demanding, invalidating, rejecting, or blaming.

To see how destructive behaviors might initiate the cycle of anger in romantic relationships, let us imagine the following scenario: Partner A and B have financial problems. One day, A comes home from work to find B drinking a very expensive alcoholic beverage. Furious and instead of giving B a chance to explain, A resorts to destructive behaviors (e.g., name-calling). See Fig. 2, middle section, top rectangle.

At this juncture, what might fuel the cycle of anger is B's accurate perception of A's behavior. Is there a high likelihood that B will correctly perceive the destructiveness in A's behavior? Yes. According to previous research, romantic partners are good at identifying each other's conflict-related response styles. So B can easily tell whether A is being hostile or providing constructive criticism. The cycle of anger usually continues down Path C (Fig. 2, right side), because Partner A's antagonistic behavior, once correctly perceived by Partner B, elicits B's anger. It is natural that B would feel angry, because when people sense that others are rejecting them (instead of responsive and supportive), they feel indignant. Note that this path we have been following—from A to B to C—could be initiated by the other partner too (Figure 1, starting from the bottom right corner and moving left). Just as Partner A's anger can result in A behaving destructively, Partner B's anger might also motivate B to behave in a destructive manner. Therefore, the cycle can be set in motion from different points. But the results might be the same: perpetuating the cycle of destructive behavior and anger and intensifying negative emotions and abusive actions—perhaps to a point where neither partner recalls the initial source of anger which set this destructive cycle of rage in motion.

Sisters, can I serve you fair warning. The decision to marry and to accept a lifelong companion is not a decision to be made on our own. Contrary to popular belief, we should not keep everyone out of our business. This is a time for community, especially if we decide to marry young. Our community can ask questions that we may not consider. The concept that love is blind, takes on a new meaning since love and infatuation may cause us to ignore signs that point to danger. And if we choose to have sex before marriage it further complicates things and causes our vision to become obscured. That's because we begin to view most things through the lens of lust and eroticism opposed to logic and Christian perspective. Although healthy and fulfilling sex is vital to a thriving marriage, it is merely one component. That being said, if we are being physically, emotionally, and spiritually depleted and abused, it will take a toll on our libido as well.

For those of us who may be considering marriage, here is a guideline that I developed to help identify some of the basics.

Nugget: *Be prepared for God to change our desires. He has a sneaky way of doing that.*

1. *Desires*: In this column, we will list every desire that we have in a potential husband. Let's be as superficial and detailed as we choose. A girl can dream, right? Please note that it is common and expected that these desires will change with age, as well as natural and spiritual maturity.

2. *Compromise*: In this column, start to look over at the "Desires" list and ask yourself, "Can I live without this?" For example, if I listed five feet eleven inches, light skin, and freckles, and I believe that I could live a healthy and fulfilled marriage in the absence of these traits, I would also write them in the compromise column. But if I believe that failure to have these traits will cause me to look at my husband with disdain or that I would fantasize about the desires that I compromised on, it is safe to say that I should not compromise.

3. *Will not tolerate*: In this column, list all the things that you would not tolerate in a relationship. Please consider the list of mental health symptoms as a guideline. Try to avoid

forcing things to fit. For example, at times, we may look at a dysfunctional, nonmarital relationship that we are or were in and choose to omit things from our "will not tolerate" list because we do not want to accept that our current relationship is not working. If you are displaying psychopathology at all, that means you cannot adequately tolerate it. We should *never* deviate from our will not tolerate list. Meaning, if someone has traits that fit in this column, and you choose to engage in spite of that, your emotional and physical health will likely be compromised and based on one's ability to cope, it could be a threat to your physical safety. Another example, let's say that you cannot tolerate someone who cheats, lies, or steals. You will never be able to tolerate this, if you changed your mind, it would most likely be because you have lowered your standards and are now operating in codependency or in an invalid state.

4. *What I have to offer*: In this column, we get to brag on God by listing all the wonderful qualities that he has instilled in us. Yes, even the physical qualities.

Boundaries are not only reserved for romantic relationships. They are necessary in all aspects of our lives and should function smoothly in all of our other relationships including our girlfriends, our children, our ministries, places of business, and family, including our parents and elders. We will explore a few of these other areas in *friends, family, and foes.*

As we continue to explore boundaries, let's review some things that we have already covered and begin to talk techniques. After all, we already know that we have significant problems, what we lack is the skill to do anything about them.

This next segment will touch on the idea of self-care, a concept that deserves a section of its own. There is a Chinese proverb that reads, "Give a man a fish and he will eat for a day. Teach a man to fish and he will eat for a lifetime." Show of hands, how many of us once believed that this was a Bible verse?

Boundary violations tend to perpetuate themselves for varying reasons, but here are a few:

1. We believe that we are helping others by doing something for someone as opposed to that person doing something for themselves.
2. We lack the ability or courage to say no.
3. We operate in codependence.

Consider the number of times that you may have said yes to someone when your head and heart actually said no? How many times have you asked yourself, "How do I always find myself in these situations?" or "Seriously, again? I said I was not going to do this to myself anymore." And yet, here we are, attempting to manage our emotions.

As we consider our emotions and the behaviors that follow, it's probably, at least for many of us reading, it's time to do something different.

As women, we tend to carry the burdens of others, often without giving second thought to our own needs or desires. Or contrarily, we know that things may be too much for us to handle, yet we take them on anyway.

For an activity, read the role of a different kind of beast, a service animal referred to as a donkey. Then compare any similarities between a donkey and yourself. Be sure to notate your findings.

According to American Donkey and Mule Society, donkeys may be used to or for:

1. Help families with household chores and labor such as fetching water and firewood
2. Recreational riding, recreational driving, both single and in teams
3. Transport household members and/or their goods; to carry the heavy load since the animals walk at about a human's foot pace and are such enjoyable companions on the trail

4. Carry such items on its back in panniers if that is more convenient than pulling it

Fig. 3. dedMazay. "Donkey carries a large bag, raster." *Shutterstock*, n.d., https://www.shutterstock. com/image-illustration/donkey-carries-large-bag-raster-89568121?src=f5ucbaaXfxa_ysA9-vaJrQ-1-19. Accessed 14 Apr 2019

Were you shocked to learn that we often operate in roles meant for a service animal or beast of labor? Let's compare the similarities (see table 3):

Table 3. Comparison of Roles for Women and Donkeys

Women	Donkey
Helps her family to manage and complete tasks such as household chores Brings water and food as needed	Help families with household chores and labor such as fetching water and firewood
She is the caravan driver and transportation specialist She drives individuals and teams of children and adults to all necessary appointments	Recreational riding, recreational driving, both single and in teams

She carries the emotional and physical burdens of her loved ones Including secrets, back packs, laundry baskets and grocery bags	Transport household members and/or their goods to carry the heavy load since the animals walk at about a human's foot pace and are such enjoyable companions on the trail

No wonder we are upset most of the time; we are burdened. We have somehow abandoned our crown as princesses and taken on the role of a beast instead.

In order to effectively manage our emotions and keep big brother, a.k.a. our beast at bay, it's time to start saying no. Of course, we cannot say no to everything, and if you are not accustomed to saying no, this will be a difficult feat. So, let's instead begin by reserving our yes for things that actually serve us.

When making a decision to say yes or no, there are several points to consider. We should ask ourselves:

1. Is this something that I desire to do?
2. Is this my issue/responsibility or am I being a donkey? (Don't rely on memory, refer back to varying roles of a donkey.)
3. Is this task realistic based on time, ability, etc.?
4. Is my yes cheating someone out of a learning or life experience? (Consider the Chinese proverb.)
5. Is my yes making me feel depleted or taken advantage of?
6. Am I being codependent? If no, who does this benefit, and how, specifically?

It is also important to:

1. Empower others to take things to God. Instead of doing the work for them provide resources. (Refer again to the Chinese proverb.)
2. When no is necessary, an explanation is not always necessary. (We will discuss this more in the effective communication section.)

3. Know the difference between charity and obligation.
4. Saying no requires practice, seriously!

Nugget: *Practice makes permanent.*

Just for fun, how would you respond?

It's Friday and a good friend calls you first thing in the morning in need of a babysitter. She explains that she won two tickets to a sold-out concert, and she and a mutual friend plan to go. She knows that you "enjoy staying in and relaxing" on Friday nights and likely had no plans. You do not want to babysit. Using the decision-making steps above, how would you address this?

Now that we have begun to identify the need for boundaries in our lives, let's now consider the ideology of healthy boundaries as the gateway to holistic healing. I have found that there are three areas in our lives where boundaries are most important: Our emotional boundaries, physical (personal or spatial) boundaries, and boundaries in our spiritual life. Here is another opportunity for us to do some work.

Begin by listing three things in each category that deplete us, and by us, I mean Y-O-U.

This is a personal matter, and all irritants are not created equal. Meaning, what bothers one person may not necessarily bother the next, and, that too, is quite natural. Here are some examples of boundary violations:

- Someone yelling at you may deplete you emotionally.
- Someone standing too closely may violate personal boundaries because it makes you feel uncomfortable.
- Someone interrupting your personal prayer time or minimizing or devaluing your style of worship may be a spiritual violation.

These may all be things that cause you to feel stressed, depressed, and even angry. Go ahead and list your own examples in the table below or in a notebook of your choice (see table 4).

Table 4. Emotional, Physical, and Spiritual Triggers

Emotional	Physical	Spiritual
People who chronically complain	Lack of sleep	Being too busy for personal devotion
Clingy or needy people who are not my clients		Someone interrupting my personal prayer time
Liars		

Now, when it comes to establishing boundaries, here are several points to consider:

1. We must first define our limits, but we can't set good boundaries if we're uncertain about what we want or need. As women of faith, we must consult our creator through prayer. Meditation, which is listening for the voice of God, and journaling are also great ways to determine what we need.
2. Next, we must identify our physical, emotional, and spiritual limits.

   Use the above table as a guideline. Begin to consider what you can tolerate and accept versus what makes you feel uncomfortable or stressed. These feelings also help us to identify what our limits are in each of these areas.
3. Don't ignore your emotions, but don't allow them to govern you either.
   - Check in with your emotions to determine truth.
   - Ask yourself, "What is causing the feelings?"
   - What is it about the situation that is causing you discomfort or grief?
   - Can it be changed or is it about acceptance?
4. Rest is vital! Poor sleep hygiene can lead to or exacerbate mental health or physical ailments.
5. Give yourself permission to set boundaries. Boundaries are both natural and healthy. Setting them is a sign of self-respect.

6. Make self-care a priority. If you consider God in all that you do and schedule yourself second only to him, you will have the desire and the energy to attend to others. Remember, self-care also includes nurturing your spirit and caring for your body. That means you have to continue using your Christian coping skills.
7. Be assertive; say no when necessary.
8. Never violate your own boundaries. Maintain your boundaries OR set yourself up for constant irritation, distraction, and an inability to operate in your purpose. Because we, as women, are natural help meets, we will be tempted to bend our boundaries, but before you violate your own boundaries, Stop and ASSESS:
   - *Ask* yourself, what has changed that supports your decision to remove the boundary? Ask yourself if you are being pressured to change your mind or have your desires changed.
   - *Speak* up about violations right away.
   - *Shift* break the monotony. It's important to change things up occasionally, or you may suffer from boredom. Boredom leads to boundary violations. This may include friends and events. Try something fresh and exciting without compromising your beliefs.
   - *Express* yourself when appropriate and necessary. If something is painful, hurtful or annoying, don't hold it in solely to save face or because your emotions make others uncomfortable. Take a mental survey of the people and tasks that consume most of your time and energy, then begin to assess whether they should remain. Ask yourself if it's worth your peace.
   - *Stop* doing things that cause you pain or contention. *Stop* suffering alone, seek professional psychological help.
   - *Seek* a licensed Christian psychotherapist who aligns with your foundation and Christian beliefs. If one is not in your area or he or she is not a good fit, don't allow that to deter you. Find another licensed therapist.

Nugget: *It is not enough to create boundaries, follow through is everything. Others may not appreciate our boundaries, but if we uphold them, others will respect them.*

Effective Communication

If we stop to consider the things that cause many problems in our lives, communication is likely at the top of the list. Communication is something that we use every day without thinking about it, and that is where the issue lies. As one who teaches effective communication, I venture to say that we should not say anything without first considering the cost.

If talk is cheap, as the adage implies, then why does it cost us our relationships?

Whatever we say, do, and fail to say or do, we, as the person communicating, are conveying a message that is intended for the receiver. Here are some steps that I have come up with:

First, the receiver decodes what is being said.

Second, the receiver weighs it against what is not being said.

Third, the receiver factors in other distinguishing components in order to translate the message.

We will further dissect these components in a few moments. But if the message is deemed inflammatory, it may be very costly indeed. In fact, failure to communicate effectively can lead to a dissatisfying, unfruitful life.

So what is communication? Communication, in its most simplistic form, is sending a message from one person to another. The difficult and often confusing thing about communication is that communicating involves more than just words. Communication is primarily comprised of three major components: words, tone, and body language.

- *Words*: What the sender literally verbalized. This refers to the actual words that were said.

- *Tone*: This includes tone of voice, i.e., inflection and which words the sender chose to stress.
- *Body language*: This includes our posture, stance, and facial expressions.

For example, "I didn't say you were stupid" can be interpreted in multiple ways. Let's say each sentence aloud so that we can gain clarity regarding the importance of inflection as it relates to communication.

1. "I didn't *say* you were stupid."

    The implication here is that the speaker never actually verbalized that the receiver was stupid; however, based on the inflection on the word say, it was certainly implied.
2. "*I* didn't say you were stupid."

    Here, the sender is essentially implying that someone did say that the receiver was stupid. But they are saying that they are not the one who said it. This statement is laced in sarcasm.
3. I didn't say *you* were stupid.

    Can we agree, it is evident that someone was called stupid here? It is now left to the receiver to try and discern who that someone is.
4. "I didn't say you were *stupid*."

    Okay, if not stupid, then what? An idiot maybe? Again, this statement is inflammatory due to its implication.

Did you notice how each of the sentences stressed a different word and portrayed an entirely different message?

The question is, how can someone distinguish what we mean? Well, our bodies, our nonverbal communication tends to speak for us. It's a term defined as "emotional leakage."

According to Ekman, "Emotional leakage refers to emotional information that we pass on to others through our body language. This information might be conveyed unintentionally, through a threatening gaze, a haughty stare, or a cold or aloof manner. These micro-expressions may be fleeting, but audiences are able to detect them." Ekman went further to state that although these micro-expressions occur involuntarily within a fraction of a second, they tend to expose someone's true emotions.

If we are not keenly aware and intentional about the congruence of our words compared to our body language, our emotional leakage will depict a much different message than what we intended. To further complicate communication, there are other factors as it relates to interpreting body language. One that is important to note is culture.

As an African American woman, we tend to be very passionate and animated. Whether we are expressing ourselves in a positive or negative manner, our voices tend to rise, fluctuate in varying octaves, and our hands begin to flail. There seems to be an unwritten code that helps black women to decipher when another black woman is angry, when things are going awry, when she is narrating a story, or when she is simply excited and expressing herself in a celebratory fashion. Because we are demonstrative, others who are not culturally astute may easily misinterpret our passion as a black woman, and it becomes miscommunicated as aggression.

Now, it may seem unjust, but it is certainly wise for all women to remain cognizant of their own body language and cultural norms as they interact with others, especially when it comes to others who do not share the same culture. Depending on the setting, we may need to "code switch" as deemed appropriate. Code switching, in this instance, refers to "switching from one accepted vocabulary, cadence, style, or set of rules to another" (Skiba).

In many instances, we code switch naturally. For example, during a job interview, our professional voice instinctively kicks into gear. Our telephone voice automatically shifts on the second that we learn we are speaking to someone of importance, or our tones and mannerisms change whenever we are addressing someone of authority such as a police officer or someone we perceive as intelligent or in a position of power. In other cases, such as interaction with close friends, peers, or family members, there is little need for code switching since those we are familiar with tend to speak or be familiar with the code.

This brings us back to our anger. When dealing with conflict, it is vital that we all utilize the ability to code switch and minimize body language that may be perceived as dismissive, cavalier, or aggressive. Failure to do so may lead to undue conflict. And in the case of black women, our body language may be erroneously viewed as being the angry black girl in the room.

Sticks and Stones

As a child, we had these silly chants, "Sticks and stones may break my bones, but words will never hurt me" and "I am rubber and you are glue, whatever you say, bounces off of me and sticks to you!" As adults, we know that these statements could not be further from the truth. The truth is, sticks and stones will break our bones and words can leave emotional scars for a lifetime. I personally believe these were lies that our parents told us to make us feel better about our so-called friends. A word misspoken or verbal abuse as identified in chapter 1 can lead to:

- Poor self esteem
- Poor self-worth
- Lack of empathy for others
- Failure to thrive

Verbal Infractions and Violations

Words are powerful! In fact, the Bible says that "the power of life and death are in the tongue" (Prov. 18:21). Throughout our lifetimes, we may have been called names or told things about ourselves that have led to emotional scars. I refer to this as a verbal infraction. Verbal infractions are any words that diminish or violate one's self-esteem or self-worth.

Here is a list of deprecating statements that I have heard from women who I have counselled over the years. As we review this list of verbal infractions outlined below; begin to take personal inventory of any words or behaviors that may have been ascribed to you, as well as words that you may have inflicted on others. You may have some other things that you can add to this list.

- Someone cursing and or yelling at you
- Being called stupid, fat, skinny, or ugly
- Devaluing and degrading statements such as, "I don't know why I even waste my time on you"
  - You want to be or do what? LOL! Well, good luck
  - Don't even bother trying, it's too hard, you won't get it
  - You/She's got a screw loose
  - You're/She's not playing with a full deck
  - You/She's out to lunch
  - Dumb blonde
  - Air head
  - Lights on, but no one is home
  - Nobody asked you, you don't know anything
  - You're cute for a fat girl
  - You're/She's cute, but you/she has no shape, or you're/she's flat chested
  - That's for smart girls, skinny girls, pretty girls, etc.
  - Why are you wasting your time on that? No one in our family has ever done that before, don't even bother trying, you won't get it
  - What's wrong with you, are you crazy or something
  - Crazy/Stupid B_ _ _h!!

We may be surprised as we begin to realize how words have impacted us. We may not have realized that the way we view ourselves was actually someone else's idea that we adapted over time. Take a few moments to consider how these or other words have affected the decisions that you have made or the relationships that you have chosen.

When God provided illumination about my past relationships and connected it back to my childhood scars, I was in disbelief. I had adapted a belief about myself and my worth based upon the words of bullies and, though my dad did not realize it, he cosigned and validated these beliefs. This makes me wonder about the ideas that he adapted about himself.

I know it is often difficult to look at hurtful things from our past because we desire to stay in the moment. However, as we consider the anatomy of anger and begin our journey to healing and resolve, it may be necessary to take inventory of our past and make amends with the princess within. It's time that we minister to the little girl inside and begin to nurture her, love her, and encourage her. Perhaps it's necessary to spend some time learning from our past, consider how it has impacted our present, and begin to actively shift things for our future.

To do so, we must begin to tackle the tough questions. The first being: Does it matter who said the words that caused you pain? If so, why and to what magnitude? My answer would be absolutely; it matters. The words from my dad caused me the most pain because I looked to him for validation, and his validation paved the way for all other relationships. Please do not misunderstand me; I am not blaming my dad for the way that my life unfolded. I am saying that my perspective regarding how he viewed me caused me to seek gratification in other men.

The more I get to know myself, the better my life becomes. I understand that words hurt! I can attempt to deceive myself by saying, "I don't care what he or she says," but that does not serve me well, and my emotional leakage defies me by its inability to keep a secret. I have learned that the offense is greater, and injuries are more severe for me when it comes from the men in my life.

Although I have forgiven my father for calling me Fuzzy Wuzzy, it continues to have some impact on my life. The hurt has found its way into my marriage and robs my husband the pleasure of watching his wife comb her hair or run his fingers through my coils. That's because I find myself bracing for impact; I find myself waiting for the insult. As a result, when I notice him watching me, I shy away. When he reaches out to stroke my hair, I pull away, find a reason to leave the room, avoid his embrace, or challenge his reasons for looking at me.

This can easily become an argument if I don't address the root of the issue. I find myself being irritated by his displays of affection, which leads to tension between us both. I often wonder how different my romantic relationships would be if I didn't wear the scars of my past. But they tend to haunt me every day. Still believe talk is cheap?

Communication Styles

If we've heard it once, we've heard it a thousand times: the key to a good relationship is communication. Communication. Communication! But please don't think that communication only applies to our romantic relationships. It's quite the contrary. Good communication is the key to all relationships including our platonic, parental, interpersonal, business, and ministry relationships.

Have you ever tried to establish or maintain a relationship with someone who did not bother to mince words? Instead, they gave you a piece of their mind, or the raw, uncut version without consideration for your feelings? Or perhaps you have been told that you are the one with a "strong personality." And when people reference you, they begin with a disclosure such as, "I love her, but," or "She really is a sweet girl, however," or they find the need to constantly defend your character by saying, "You just have to get to know her." These are often indicators that we are difficult to get along with and that our communication style either needs a makeover or a complete overhaul.

I think we can agree that we often know what we desire to say. But due to lack of skill, the approach mangles the message. Now, I'm sure I'm not the only one who has desired to say one thing that may have seemed brilliant as I considered it in my mind, but once the words slipped from my lips, there were casualties. Sisters, have your lips ever betrayed you by saying aloud a thought you meant to keep concealed in your mind? If so, you are in good company. As my mother often says, "Come back here, what I said!" If only retracting or redacting a statement were that easy.

Communication is a behavior that needs to be intentionally positive until being kind becomes second nature. This takes practice and, remember, practice makes permanent.

When learning to communicate effectively, we must first consider and rehearse the message that we wish to send. Doing so may also include plausible outcomes. We must also say exactly what we mean and mean exactly what we say. This is not easy since emotions always play a role in communication.

In order to manage our emotions and communicate effectively without harming others, we should consider the 3Ns, another concept that I've coined. We must ask ourselves, is it *nice*, is it *necessary*, and does it *need editing*?

- *Nice*: The questions we should ask ourselves here is:
    a. Is what I am about to say nice?
    b. How would I feel if someone said it to me?
    c. If it's not nice, *stop* and ask yourself why you are saying it.
        i. Am I responding out of a place of pain?
        ii. Am I trying to prove a point?
            Is the point that I am trying to prove worth the potential cost of losing or impairing my relationship?
        iii. Am I being intentionally hurtful?
    d. If you said yes to any of the above, *stop*! *Do not* say it. Nothing positive transpires from this.
- *Necessary*: There are times that things are not considered nice, but they may be necessary for the sake of the relationship or someone's well-being. For example, if someone has bad breath, their parenting skills are questionable, or they have an abrasive personality, which causes interpersonal conflict; it may be necessary to speak up about this. Most of us would take offense if we are on the receiving end of these conversations.

    Honestly, no one wants to hear these things, but it may be necessary for our own well-being. Things that are not considered nice but are deemed necessary require more wisdom and finesse in order for the message to be received. This is because we must consider who benefits from the conversation.

For example, ask yourself the following questions:

1. Am I saying this for my own benefit if so, why?
2. Am I being violated by this person?
3. What outcome am I hoping for as a result of this conversation?
4. What is the possible impact of me saying this to someone?"

Remember the concept of outcome thinking that we learned about in chapter 1. What is the possible outcome of me saying this, will it make things better or worse? As we can see, we are searching for motive. And before you go there, of course motive matters. If our motives are impure or otherwise self-serving as opposed to being for the benefit of the relationship or growth, emotional leakage may cause this conversation to go awry. Besides, if this is a "me (you)" issue then this is a conversation that should take place with a therapist, God, or ourselves, instead.

And finally:

• *Does it need editing*: After careful consideration has been given about what needs to be said and whether it is necessary, it's now time to edit and package it correctly. Keeping in mind that the message is for the receiver, if we have a relationship with this person let's consider their capacity for this information and the best way to present the information to obtain a favorable response.

Using the example about someone having bad breath, if we said, "Ew! Your breath stinks! Did you brush your teeth today?" Or what if we begin to wave a hand demonstratively in front of our face to insinuate that something is malodourous? We have already violated the first two steps since the way we presented the message was neither nice nor necessary. Alternatively, if we pull someone aside privately and hand them a breath mint, nothing more really needs to be said. Might their ego be bruised a bit? Perhaps, but there was no intent to cause harm. Sometimes, the truth hurts. The same could be said if someone presents a bad idea. I don't tell them, "That was stupid," although I may have been thinking it. Instead, I should choose a gentler approach. By asking, "Have you considered doing it this way?" or asking what other approaches they have tried, they know that I am considering them, and they also begin to become aware that their way is not working well for them, for others, and it was not a good idea.

There are also times when a more direct approach is warranted like in the case of abuse, or intolerance for something. Even so, this should be determined on a case-by-case basis. We must broach the topic in an assertive manner with this concept in mind—"I don't want to hurt you, and I don't want you to hurt me"—instead, we are both looking for resolve. We will discuss assertive communication next as we explore the four main communication styles.

According to an article published by Princeton University, there are four main styles of communication. Although we tend to use different styles of communication depending upon the situation, most of us have a default communication style that is most dominant. The four types of communication that we will discuss are passive, passive aggressive, aggressive, and assertive.

Passive

Passive communication refers to communication behaviors that favor the needs of others at our own expense. While we may initially refer to this behavior as being benevolent and Christlike, passivity leads to resentment.

Some common traits in passive communicators are:

1. Making the choice to hold and harbor feelings as opposed to verbalizing infractions.

2. Avoiding eye contact.
3. May look to the floor while talking.
4. Often considers others and rarely considers self.

The concept associated with this behavior is anxiety-based. "If I say how I really feel or tell them no, they won't like me, or I will lose their friendship." Or "I don't want to cause any conflict, so I will choose to ignore it, maybe they will notice their behaviors on their own without me saying anything."

Passive Aggressive

Passive aggressive communication refers to communication that is laced with sarcasm and manipulation. The concept associated with this communication style is, "I really want to say no, but I lack the courage to be direct so, I will be sarcastic and irritable instead." My husband calls this "Nice Nasty."

Some common traits in passive aggressive communicators are:

1. Appearing passive on the surface, but subtly acting out in anger.
2. Exerting control over others by using sarcasm and indirect communication, or avoiding the conversation.
3. Limited consideration for the rights, needs, or feelings of others.
4. Avoids phone calls or texts, and later denies ever receiving the message.
5. Waits for others to do it so they won't have to.
6. Acts or pretends to be confused to evade accountability.
7. Intentionally sabotaging the efforts of others while pretending to be unaware of the impact.

Aggressive

Aggressive communication refers to a style of communication that is dismissive, alienating, and has little or no regard for others. Those who communicate using this style often hold the belief that their way is the most effective way and that compromise is unnecessary.

Some common traits in aggressive communicators are:

1. Exerting one's own agenda at the expense of others.
2. Stage-hogging behaviors, which disallows others from talking, failure to take turns in a conversation, or over-talking others.
3. Aggressive bullying-type behaviors, including posturing/intimidation and yelling.
4. Hurts others in the process of getting needs met.
5. May describe self as "blunt."
6. People may describe you as having a "strong personality."

Assertive

Assertive communication refers to a style of communication that is direct, honest, and that is respectful of yourself and others. Assertive communicators strive to find resolve quickly with as little collateral damage as possible.

Some common traits in assertive communicators are:

1. Having a win-win attitude.
2. Allowing others to engage in the conversation.
3. Use of active listening, without stage hogging or the need to be right.
4. Taking responsibility for her own actions.
5. Congruence between words and body language.

Speaking of communication styles, this brings me to another memory in my mid-teenage years. We were sitting down for our traditional family dinner—all seven of us—and the tension was thick in the room. Everyone was quietly dining; our forks hitting the plate were the only sounds in the room. It was obvious that something wasn't right. I can't recall what Mom said to prompt the response from my dad, but he abruptly slammed his hands down unto the table and said, "Well, excuse the hell out of me, Ruby!" That was the first and only time that I heard my father curse, and we were astonished. I witnessed our parents fight, but I never ever heard them use profanity.

After we became teenagers, my parents had long passed the stage where they were physically abusive to each other. From that time forward, we knew our parents were arguing whenever Dad would make condescending remarks like, "Well, praise the Lord, Sister Fields," or Mom would sarcastically refer to Daddy as "Deacon." Can you identify the communication style that my parents were using?

The power of influence is a force to be reckoned with. Following in my parents' footsteps, I, in turn, became the queen of cynical remarks. I began to reciprocate my parents' passive aggressive communication style. And as you recall, it cost me far more than relationships. My passive aggressive tendencies contributed to the continuation of explosive conversations that resulted in violence. I thank God that through the utilization of Christian coping skills and mental health counseling, I can effectively articulate my needs and break the cycle of abuse in my lineage.

Although I still have negative thoughts, I arrest them and make the choice to use my mouth for worship instead of war.

Here is how the author summarizes the four communication styles:

> Assertive communication is most likely to lead to respectful and longer-term relationships, so that's the style to strive for in most situations. However, passive and aggressive communication might work better on some occasions. For example, if you are feeling fearful that you are about to be harmed, passive communication may help to defuse the situation and aggressive communication might prevent the problem from getting worse. While the passive communication style can be helpful, when people pair it with subtle

aggression, the passive-aggressive style is likely to interfere with or undermine healthy relationships (Princeton University).

As we close out this segment, remember there is no one absolute, right way when it comes to communication. But a good rule of thumb is to abide by the golden rule as depicted in Luke 6:31, "Do unto others as you would have them to do unto you."

Becoming a Square: Avoiding Toxic Circles

Satan is attractive, alluring, appealing, and also very subtle. In Ephesians 2:2, Paul refers to him as the "prince and power of the air" and the spirit that entices "the children of disobedience." The name Satan was given to Lucifer after his fall from grace and it literally means adversary. An adversary is an enemy and an opposer—one who fights and contends in direct combat against another force. His sole desire is to derail the children of God and to cause us to find fault in our Lord and Savior.

Job 1: 1–7 reads:

> One day the sons of God came to present themselves before the LORD, and Satan also came with them. "Where have you come from?" said the LORD to Satan. "From roaming through the earth," he replied, "and walking back and forth in it." Then the LORD said to Satan, "Have you considered my servant Job? For there is no one on earth like him, a man who is blameless and upright, who fears God and shuns evil." Satan answered the LORD, "Does Job fear God for nothing? Have You not placed a hedge on every side around him and his household and all that he owns? You have blessed the work of his hands, and his possessions have increased in the land.

But stretch out Your hand and strike all that he
has, and he will surely curse You to Your face."

Before I say another word here, I have to acknowledge that
my response would have been, "Wait...what? Lord, I was minding
my own business staying in my own lane. Why make an example of
me?" But when I consider that the earth is the Lord's and the fullness thereof as are the world and those who dwell therein, conviction
silences me. God—as the architect of the universe—owns the right to
make decisions on behalf of his creation. Besides, could you imagine
God having that level of faith in you? To say, "Take your best shot,
this one is mine, and she will not capitulate, no matter the price."

In the passage, Satan is suggesting that we serve the Lord solely
for financial and personal gain, and he vehemently plots for us to
discredit and dismiss God and ultimately renounce our position
as heirs to the throne of God our father. To do so is, by default, a
choice to spend eternity in damnation. Hell was created for Satan
and his angels. However, due to the perversion of man, "hell has
enlarged herself" in order to accommodate the vast number of occu-
pants, which is those of us who have chosen to occupy hell, instead of
the kingdom of God that has been prepared for us (Isa. 5:14, Matt.
25:41, John 14:3).

The Word of God continues to caution us to be vigilant about
the enemy and his devices, and sinful men, "Lest we be swept away"
(Num. 16:26). However, based on what we learned in chapter 2
"Exploring the Woman of Faith," only half of Christians read the
Word of God. Sisters, it's no wonder we are being tossed to and fro
by the waves of life. Who brings a knife to a pistol war? Well, appar-
ently, we do.

Contrary to popular belief, Satan is not omnipotent (all-power-
ful), he is not omnipresent (in all places, at all times), and he is not
omniscient (all-knowing), but he is powerful, and his kingdom is
undivided. Due to our disobedience to the mandates of God, many
Christians are rendered powerless! In contrast to walking in power
and authority as agents and disciples of God, we are bound. We are
enslaved and burdened by depression, overcome with anxiety, and

held captive by bad decisions, guilt, cyclic sin, generational curses, and toxic relationships.

We wonder why we can't fight or ward off these things, but we can! The Word of God tells us that we can do all things through him who gives us strength (Phil. 4:13). Ephesians 6:11–17 admonishes us to:

> Put on the whole armor of God that ye may be able to stand against the wiles of the devil. For we wrestle not against flesh and blood, but against principalities, against powers, against the rulers of the darkness of this world, against spiritual wickedness in high places. Wherefore take unto you the whole armor of God that ye may be able to withstand in the evil day, and having done all, to stand. Stand therefore, having your loins girt about with truth, and having on the breastplate of righteousness; And your feet shod with the preparation of the gospel of peace; Above all, taking the shield of faith, wherewith ye shall be able to quench all the fiery darts of the wicked. And take the helmet of salvation, and the sword of the Spirit, which is the word of God.

So, what's the problem, given what the word of God offers us? Could the reason for our lack of power be due to our own passivity? Or is it that we are trying to live a Christian life without Christ? If so, well, in the words of my husband, Pastor Tobaise Brookins, "You want to do things your own way and remove God from the equation? Well, good luck, 'cause you gonna' need all the luck you can get!" Home girl, you haven't a prayer.

Listen, I don't know about you, but I was sick and tired of my purpose being pimped out by the devil. I was utterly and completely over being disgruntled, confused, and strung out. I was operating out of a place of toxicity, chasing this phantom referred to as passion. The only place my passion led me was to the road of destruction.

"Follow your heart!" they say, but the Word of God says that the heart is desperately wicked (Jer. 17:9). So again, I urge us all to consider whether or not we are trying to live a Christian life without Christ! It certainly appears so, and our lives reflect the choices that we have made.

I pray that you know my heart by now and can discern that this is not intended to excite guilt. And it is by no means meant to be judgmental. Remember our adversary—the prince and power of the air—is very cunning so it's easy to get caught up. Trust me, I get it. I've been there and done that three times. I truly believe that the Lord has charged me to talk about the difficult matters. I know that my life purpose is to use my testimony from hurt to healing to assist others to navigate through difficult, perilous times. And because religious folks have thrown me unto the proverbial altar and defined me as unfit to be used by God, I have been sent to teach about the mercy and redemptive power of our Lord and Savior.

If he was able to redeem me—a serial wife, self-righteous, rebellious, jailbird—he can certainly redeem you. Just as the Lord knew that Job would refuse to curse him no matter the pressure, he also knew that once he redeemed me from a life riddled with sin and shame that I would not be ashamed to talk about it. Though I did not understand the journey, the Lord was operating beyond my ability to understand. While I was busy blowing out of marriages, my Heavenly Father was rehabilitating, developing, maturing, and grooming Tobaise to cover me. It was always my fate to be a pastor's wife. It is part of my destiny to be a therapist recovering from the ails of life. For it is these things that provided me with a platform to do the perfect will of God.

If we are not careful, our season of hardship can become a lifetime of pain. And what was intended to challenge and matriculate us becomes a deterrent from our purpose instead. "For wide is the gate and broad is the road that leads to destruction, and many enter through it. But small is the gate and narrow the road that leads to life, and only a few find it" (Matt. 7:13–14). So, my Kingdom sisters, this is absolutely not a persecutory message. Rather, this is a message of love that unveils the enemy's plan and conjures change.

Because it is vital to understand our enemy, here are a few final points about Satan. I believe that we ignorantly minimize the influence of Satan over our lives. He is no one to play with, and the power that he can have over us should not be diminished. The Bible portrays Satan in several ways, i.e., powerful, deceptive, a liar, subtle, a thief, and as an accuser of the brethren, just to name a few.

Powerful: "Be sober, be watchful: your adversary the Devil, as a roaring lion, walks about, seeking whom he may devour" (1 Pet. 5:8).

A deceiver: "Put on the whole armor of God, that you may be able to stand against the wiles of the Devil" (Eph. 6:11). See also Revelation 12.

A liar: "You belong to your father, the devil, and you want to carry out your father's desires. He was a murderer from the beginning, not holding to the truth, for there is no truth in him. When he lies, he speaks his native language, for he is a liar and the father of lies" (John 8:44).

Subtle: "But I fear, lest by any means, as the serpent beguiled Eve in his craftiness, your minds should be corrupted from the simplicity and the purity that is toward Christ" (2 Cor. 11:3).

A thief: "The thief comes only to steal and kill and destroy; I have come that they may have life and have it to the full" (John 10:10).

An accuser: Revelation 12:7–12 (see below).

> And there was war in heaven: Michael and his angels fought against the dragon; and the dragon fought and his angels, and prevailed not; neither was their place found any more in heaven. And the great dragon was cast out, that old serpent, called the Devil, and Satan, which deceiveth the whole world: he was cast out into the earth, and his angels were cast out with him. And I heard a loud voice saying in heaven, Now is come salvation, and strength, and the kingdom of our God,

and the power of his Christ: for the accuser of our brethren is cast down, which accused them before our God day and night. And they overcame him by the blood of the Lamb, and by the word of their testimony; and they loved not their lives unto the death. Therefore rejoice, ye heavens, and ye that dwell in them. Woe to the inhabiters of the earth and of the sea! For the devil is come down unto you, having great wrath, because he knoweth that he hath but a short time.

I believe Satan gains strength and takes pleasure in knowing that most of us are immature Christians who are girded with a dance and a celebratory shout, rather than with truth. We have little more than vain babble with our impotent Sunday morning chants.

- "Won't he do it!"
- "Yaaaass, this is my season!"
- "The devil thought he had me!"
- "The devil is under my feet!"
- "But God!"

These chants feel good in the moment, but they equate to nothing more than lip service rather than the authority given by the sword of the spirit, which is the living word of God. We have feet that run toward things of the world as we chase every evil passion. We look to destroy our sisters hoping to excel in her stead. We have forsaken the breastplate of righteousness and have become hellions in lieu of having feet shod with the preparation of the gospel of peace.

Instead of taking the shield of faith to quench the fiery darts of the wicked, we have made our lips a place where malice dwells and our hearts a den for discontentment. We have replaced our helmet of salvation with a haughty crown of self-righteousness, arrogance, pride, and pompous self-love instead.

So, the problem isn't that we can't fight because we can! The problem is that we have replaced our armor and, by default, forfeited our crown! We have forsaken our battle gear because we assumed it was too cumbersome. We thought the breastplate was too heavy, not understanding that we need it to protect our heart. We despise our helmet of salvation, which is meant to protect our mind, thoughts, and emotions. And today, as a result, we flee unnecessarily from an already-defeated foe. The battle against Satan has already been won for us, and we can maintain that victory by holding onto our crowns and our battle gear!

As indicated earlier, the enemy is not ignorant, and his kingdom is undivided as is described in Mark 3:23–26:

> How can Satan drive out Satan? If a kingdom is divided against itself, it cannot stand. If a house is divided against itself, it cannot stand. And if Satan is divided and rises against himself, he cannot stand; his end has come. Indeed, no one can enter a strong man's house to steal his possessions unless he first ties up the strong man. Then he can plunder his house.

However, because of the structure of Satan's kingdom, we have the misguided belief that Satan is all-knowing and can see and discern all things. That is not true. What is true, however, is demonic forces have been devising a plan for our demise from our time of conception. Why? Because before the foundation of the world God already had a plan for each of us. "Before I formed you in the womb, I knew you, before you were born, I set you apart; I appointed you as a prophet to the nations" (Jer. 1:5). Therefore, the battle for our affection and purpose began.

Aborting Our Purpose

The devil wants us to abort our purpose. Medically, an abortion as defined by *Webster* is the "deliberate termination of a human pregnancy, most often performed during the first twenty-eight weeks of pregnancy." ScienceDaily defines an abortion as "the removal or expulsion of an embryo or fetus from the uterus, resulting in or caused by its death." Spiritually speaking, aborting our purpose refers to the willful termination of God's divine will and assignment for our life. We are all created differently, having our own unique set of character traits, strengths, vulnerabilities, and complex personalities. This ultimately means that we each have an individualized sphere of influence.

What I seek to convey here is that I may be able to reach a population that turns a deaf ear to you. And you may be able to draw a crowd who may be dismissive to me. And it's all a part of God's plan.

If I can be honest, wait…what am I saying? I have been transparent the entire time. But sometimes, I have a difficult time hearing someone preach or teach because they have a bad weave, they forgot to floss, or (the shame of this next statement) they had chipped nail polish. Sisters, I can be distracted by the silliest things.

Personalities are God's doing. Human flaws and all are inevitable. Our personalities make us amazing people and add to the pleasures of life. Besides, if an individual had the monopoly and complete influence on all people, there would be no need for God. Our personalities and flaws keep us humble and diligently seeking the Lord for guidance.

(Nugget: *Please do not attempt to alter your personality after you have become saved. I promise, it will come in handy.*)

We are many members of one body, all having a specific task and purpose. We labor individually and collectively with one divine purpose in mind; to spread the Gospel of Jesus Christ which includes the reproduction of disciples and advancement of God's kingdom (1 Cor. 12:12–27).

Since the enemy does not want any threat to his kingdom, he takes serious strides to disenfranchise the children of God by first enticing us to abort our purpose prior to the born-again experience. That can happen by default, omitting God's commandments from our life, or by committing outright acts that demonstrate our displeasure for God. We then ultimately abandon or "abort" our purpose.

Am I ignorant to assume that most born again believers desire to abide by the word of God and to do all that we can to uphold righteousness? Did you know that it actually becomes more difficult for the enemy to overtake and overthrow a believer once we have been born again? This is because we have the "power" of the Holy Spirit residing in us (Acts 1:8). Needless then, to say, after the infilling of the Holy Ghost, Satan becomes more diligent and strategic in his scheme to snuff out our purpose.

Let me ask you this, if the enemy showed up with horns blazing, wouldn't most of us valiantly resist? The answer is yes. Now, because Satan is wise, he changes the game plan and makes attempts to disrupt our purpose by causing us to miscarry instead of aborting it.

Miscarriage of Our Purpose

A miscarriage or spontaneous abortion is a medical term that refers to the rejection or intrauterine death of an embryo or fetus prior to a certain level of maturation. According to the Mayo Clinic, some known causes of miscarriage are serious infection, injury, or disease. As it relates to miscarrying our purpose, the enemy attempts to upset or misalign God's plan, causing us to become spiritually infected, injured, and diseased, which can result in the death of our purpose.

Infected: When I speak of spiritual infection, I am referring to the invasion and reproduction of social and emotional toxins and other harmful agents that cause us, as believers, to become spiritually sick. Sickness leads to apathy, lethargy, and overall discomfort. This may occur due to exposure to pollutants such as unhealthy relationships, gossiping, back biting (two-faced behaviors), lack of spiritual self-care and regular "check-ups" such as diligence to the word, attending worship services, reading our Bible, and prayer. By this time, these terms which are our Christian coping skills, should be quite familiar. They may even seem redundant at this point. But as followers of Christ, it's no secret that we require frequent prompts as it relates to obedience to God and his plan and purpose for our lives. Don't believe me? Let's throw back to the infamous wilderness experience outlined in Exodus chapters 1–12.

Moses declared the children of Israel "stiff-necked" because of their willful disobedience, constant murmuring, and chronic complaints regarding their own deliverance. Instead of abiding by the plan to flee captivity and inhabiting the promised land flowing with milk and honey, they chose to rebel against the prophet Moses and were ravished in the wilderness instead. This was after the Lord had caused the plagues to fall upon Egypt, all while saving the children of Israel alive. How easily, they—we (the saints)—seem to forget the commandments of the Lord.

As a result of not following the plan of God, they wandered aimlessly in the wilderness for forty years. Of the approximate 2.5 million Israelites who left out of Egypt in the book of Exodus 12, only two from the original group reached the land promised to their forefathers (Josh. 14). If left untreated or unresolved, spiritual infection can lead to stagnation, confusion, disease, and, eventually, spiritual demise.

Injured: When the Lord spoke to me about spiritual injury, "church hurt" immediately came to mind. The term church hurt has been tossed around with such frequency and in such a flip, careless manner that the emotional injury caused by the actions of careless shepherds has become no more than the grand delusion of a disgruntled parishioner.

But the ideology of church hurt is, in fact, legitimate. When we consider an injury or an infliction, pain is a common symptom. And when we are in pain, the natural tendency is to protect the sensitive area.

Think of the last time that you stubbed your toe, slammed your finger in a door, or bumped into something sharp. We instinctively grab the injured area to self-examine the damage and to prevent others from having access to it. We are protecting ourselves from further harm or intensified pain. Likewise, when we are injured in the church, often due to human error and inherent flaws that we all possess, we isolate and disallow others to gain the access necessary for close examination (conversation and explanation), which could inherently lead to our healing (resolution of the issue).

Satan understands the necessity and the power being in the presence of like-minded people. "For where two or three gather in my name, there am I with them" (Matt. 18:20). Therefore, his tactic is to divide and conquer. Satan plants the seeds that lead to isolation and isolation leads to a domino effect (see figure 4).

Fig. 4. Process of Isolation

Isolation causes the injury to go untreated, which can lead to permanent paralysis or failure to operate in the area of our spiritual gifting and purpose. We then begin to scatter ourselves (dismount, disassemble, and disunify), which creates a breach. This breach disallows us to edify and encourage one another and our purpose; therefore, our purpose ultimately dies due to our untreated injuries and isolation.

In other instances, we simply fail to live up to our full potential or purpose. We continue to minister while severely injured or wounded and spew toxicity unto others, and/or we remain in an active leadership role while we ourselves are overcome by depression, anxiety, alcoholism, sexual addiction, failing marriages and, at times, are overtaken by suicide.

Diseased: When I speak of spiritual disease, I am referring to the result of untreated spiritual infection as was defined in the aforementioned section.

Medically, the Mayo Clinic Staff states that "disease occurs when the cells in your body are damaged—as a result of the infection—and signs and symptoms of an illness appear" causing damage to the body.

As we address this from a spiritual perspective, the spirit is prone to disease via:

- *Tainted word.* False doctrine that is not biblically based or passive "watered-down" diluted teaching.
- *False prophets.* A misspoken word perceived to be from the Lord that misleads a believer.

- *Church hopping.* This refers to transient behavior. Nomads in the church who refuse to or lack the spiritual maturity or trust necessary to settle or to commit to a single place of worship or has marked difficulty submitting to leadership. A church hopper is often disgruntled, at times rebellious, prideful, and divisive, has a know-it-all attitude, is untrainable, and often forsakes membership when things are not perceived as favorable for them. Church hoppers often fail to mature spiritually or matriculate in Christendom due to lack of accountability.

Spiritual Retardation

Yes, I am aware that the phrase retardation carries a negative connotation and is now deemed as culturally insensitive or offensive. However, depicted in this manner, I do believe that it is appropriate. *Merriam-Webster* defines this dated term as "to delay or impede the development or progress of; to slow up especially by preventing or hindering advancement or accomplishment."

In addition to being a chameleon, Satan uses every weapon in his arsenal to derail us. Looking to steal, kill, and destroy the children of God for he knows that we carry purpose that brings liberation and truth. So, his final tactic is for us to have a *retarded* or stunted, underdeveloped purpose. This manifests as immature, bratty, unlearned, and powerless Christians. It's no wonder the word retarded has been deemed offensive due to the very implication of the word itself. And just as the world is offended by the word retarded, we, too, should be offended and angered by the ploy and influence that Satan has over the children of the Most High.

Spiritual retardation was not God's design, but it is a result of our own choices. The enemy rejoices over every soul that is lost. Now this, my sisters, is a reason to be fighting mad!

Sisters, I know this section was heavy, but so is our anger. Anger is a weight that can easily derail us and impact every aspect of our lives. As you begin to consider the anatomy of your own anger, you will likely find that you are entangled in toxic circles and patterns that keep you stagnant, and, like a body of water that sits too long, stagnation eventually begins to stink.

Friends, Family, Uncontracted Lovers and Foes

I want to jump-start this section by saying that life is much too short for bad friends and loving someone who does not have the capacity to love you back. Before I incite a riot, I am not discrediting the Word of God that commands us to love one another and to keep no record of wrong doings (1 Cor. 13:5). As we delve deeper into the different types of relationships and the very essence of friendship itself, things will become clearer.

But as it relates to loving someone who cannot love you back, I am speaking specifically of "Eros" erotic, sexual love, which should not be confused with "Philia" brotherly love that all Christians should possess for each other (Heb. 13:1). We will have the chance to explore the different types of love in "Balancing Life, Love, and Ministry" section.

Have you heard a preacher say that Satan desires to ruin our relationships? Well, I certainly have. I have also jumped on the bandwagon, angered and filled with righteous indignation declaring an all-out attack against the enemy! It was typically after one of those fiery services where the preacher compelled the church to "go into the enemy's camp and take back all that the devil has stolen from us!" But let's be clear, Satan is not merely looking to destroy our relationships so that we would be unhappy. Brace yourself ladies, but Satan actually takes no issue with us being happy in our relationships nor is he vexed when we are financially prosperous.

Consider celebrity couples, those who are obviously living outside of the mandates of God. I will not begin to name-drop as this guide is not meant to personally attack anyone's character nor to be judgmental, for they too are souls who need to be saved. Besides, I'm sure a few names immediately began to roll around in your mind.

When we look at their lifestyle, the money, power, fame, the millions of fans who fawn over them and create images unto them, we can see the enemy's hand in it all. Yes, Satan will allow for couples to live a lavish lifestyle and have an idealistic, coveted marriage in the eyes of man *if* it is not a threat to his kingdom. Just as the Lord has human disciples and soldiers, Satan also has an army. He has designated footmen who carry out his diabolical plan.

You see, Satan is not one of our "frenemies"—a jealous, envious girlfriend who feels inept because of our talents or jaded by the things that we possess. Sisters, we must be more mature in our Christian walk to know better than this. So, be not deceived. Satan is much more deliberate and sinister than that. Satan is in competition for our soul. An example of this is when ungodly megastars and public figures declare that they are "blessed and highly favored" and give verbal reverence to God "who is the head of their life," even though they are not abiding by the ordinance of God.

Satan already has their mind, heart, affections, and soul. Therefore, when they pay homage to Christ on a platform and the ecclesia can clearly discern that they are not living a Christian lifestyle, they do not discredit Satan.

Based on their own public displays of perversion and blatant disrespect to the written word of God, praising "God" as their "Lord and savior" is another ploy to tarnish the image of God. As it gives the illusion that sexual perversion, scantily clad women, upholding violence, and celebrating fame is an indicator of God's favor on one's life. It is a trap that keeps us engulfed in sin. And as the old mother's use to sing, "Far from the peaceful shore, very deeply stained within sinking to rise no more."

Satan could not care less about our earthly treasures, our inflated sense of fame, or our #MarriageGOALS. For him, these things are a menial exchange for the luxury of having our soul. As humans, we are captivated by success and fame, and our adversary is keenly aware of our lust for riches. It's another distraction from our purpose to keep our eyes fixed on self rather than on the things of God. The Bible warns us about paying homage to or idolizing earthy riches.

Do not store up for yourselves treasures
on earth, where moths and vermin destroy, and

where thieves break in and steal. But store up for yourselves treasures in heaven, where moths and vermin do not destroy, and where thieves do not break in and steal. For where your treasure is, there your heart will be also. (Matt. 6:19–23)

For what shall it profit a man, if he shall gain the whole world, and lose his own soul? Or what shall a man give in exchange for his soul? Whosoever therefore shall be ashamed of me and of my words in this adulterous and sinful generation; of him also shall the Son of man be ashamed, when he cometh in the glory of his Father with the holy angels. (Mark 8:36–38)

When Satan attacks our relationships and things that we hold dear to our hearts, it is because he is aware that trepidation and discord in our relationships—especially our romantic relationships—often cause us to doubt God, to stumble, or remain spiritually confused. Therefore, he attacks our relationships to get us off track. No horns here ladies; he is subtle.

I used to ask God why he allowed others to get vain glory or to use his gifts to celebrate others instead of to glorify him. But Paul answers this in Romans 11:29 by saying, "The gifts of God come without repentance." Simply put, once God gifts us with a talent or skill, he does not repossess it, as a creditor does whenever we fail to pay a debt. God gives us the free will to use the gift at our own discretion, even at the risk of us dismissing and devaluing him.

Okay, it's time to do more personal work. So, let's pick up those notebooks again. I will give fair warning. It's about to get a bit rocky. Take some time to consider the people in your life. Pay attention to people who add value versus people who cause conflict and pain, i.e., those who subtract from you. In order to protect your peace and manage your anger and emotions effectively, you must conduct careful inventory of *all* of your relationships.

I can almost see your faces now, trying to devise a plan to withhold information or leave a name off the list. It's funny how we attempt to keep God out of our business! But even devout Christians tend to trust him in every area of life except our love lives. I know that it's hard, but let's push ourselves.

The reason that this type of inventory is difficult is because it forces us to look at relationships that may be toxic or hazardous to our emotional, spiritual, and even physical health. But the conflict is that the relationship is also gratifying to some degree. This is one of the reasons that we hold on to these abusive relationships longer than we should. Some examples include an emotionally abusive friend, a dysfunctional family member, or an uncontracted, spiritually *unlawful* sexual relationship that we return to time and time again, even when the relationship does not serve us. The latter seems to be the most difficult to rid ourselves of.

In case I need to be more specific, an uncontracted, sexual relationship refers to a nonmarital relationship or any sexual relationship that has not been sanctioned by God. These are relationships that do not follow the sacrament of marriage as defined in creation and depicted in the book of Genesis chapter 2. Relationships of this kind create a wedge between us and God, and, as a result, we find ourselves in a continuous state of repentance.

Consequently, these are often the relationships that we *need* to keep tabs on, waiting and plotting for the opportunity of an unlocked and unattended phone so that we may frantically scan its history. Sound familiar? While I understand that uncontracted lovers are not everyone's plight, I am willing to wager that either you, or someone whom you love, have found themselves in this predicament at least one season of their lifetime. And if we were a good friend, we may have sat with them as they grieved for days or months *after* he left her bed for the umpteenth time even though she swore that last time was the *absolute* last time.

Pause here and ask yourself why these painful relationships are the hardest to rid yourself of. And while you are at it, ask yourself why the ones that are tethered to our hearts and every sensual part of our being keep us in emotional turmoil? If you are like me, you have already asked yourself this question a million times and, at least half of those times, you remained in the relationship, suffocating in the same emotional cesspool and slowly dying from within.

Could the reason that we continue to subject ourselves to pain by staying in an abusive relationship be that:

A. We've already invested too much time, an indispensable amount of energy, and a myriad of emotions to abandon the relationship now?
B. We want a return on our investment? Meaning that we want to get something out of it, such as an inheritance or retirement, popularity, social status, etc.
C. We have too much pride to let go?
D. We fear being alone?
E. We are driven by sexual urges?
F. We have soul ties?
G. All of the above?

The answer is, all of the above, along with a plethora of other legitimate reasons. We all have our personal reasons for staying. And again, I don't judge you for any of them no matter how foolish or superficial they may seem to others.

I interviewed eight women about their personal relationship with anger and their journey to find healing. The interviews are documented in the "Kingdom Sisters Speak" section. As I sat with each of these women, I continued to find a common thread. That regardless of our age, ethnicity, or upbringing, we had many things in common. Two of those things were that we all have the desire for protection, to love and to be loved by others, and that our abusive relationships with anger did not just simply manifest one day. We didn't wake up one morning hell-bent on being "crazy," as hurting women are typically labeled. The interviews depicted that the negative manifestation of anger (aggression) was an insidious, evolving response to an unmet need.

Maslow's hierarchy of needs outline our basic human needs, things needed for survival (see figure 5 below).

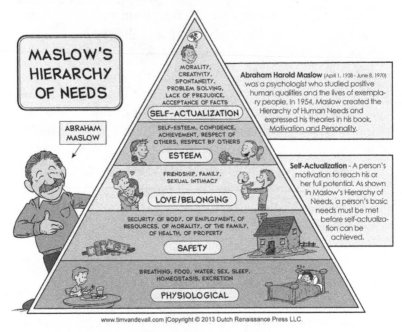

Fig. 5. Maslow's Hierarchy of Needs from: Tim's Printables.

All eight women had an unfulfilled need in one or more of these areas. While each of these women were in different parts of their journey to find healing from anger, each woman unanimously agreed that their peace was at stake and that was too high a price to pay.

So now I ask you:

1. Is the relationship worth your peace?
2. What are you willing to risk for the sake of holding on to a relationship that does not serve you or that continually causes you distress?

Although conflict in relationships is inevitable, it is manageable. Sometimes, that means you have to separate yourself from someone or learn to live with the differences between you and the ones that you love. As a reminder, conflict in itself is not the problem. Rather, it's our response to conflict that causes the problem and leads to possible destruction.

Even the best of friends and our closest family members have the innate ability to cause us distress and set our nerves on edge. Zechariah 13:6 reads, "And one shall say unto him, What are these wounds in thine hands? Then he shall answer, Those with which I was wounded in the house of my friends." Friendships naturally have disagreements, but they should not lead to strife which is bitterness, violence, and dissention.

Friendships in our inner circle are highly complex since we are emotionally attached to those who we allow to have personal access to us. It's within the confines of our inner circle—our community of friends—that our raw emotions lie. Emotions are tethered at the heart and tend to blur lines and minimize our ability to remain objective. Every time I've had to count to ten, came dangerously close to using a choice four-letter word—post salvation, mind you (still being transparent)—or asked myself if the act I was considering would damn me to hell, it was because a friend, family member, my child, or my man were aggravating me and served as the "cause." I put cause in quotes because no one causes us to react. It's our preset response to stimuli that causes us to react. That's why it is important to put our flesh under subjection (1 Cor. 9:27), commit to our Christian coping skills, and submit to the will of God. Otherwise, we would say everything that came to mind, and dangerous is the woman who says everything that comes to her mind.

Nonetheless, when we minimize objectivity, we allow our emotions to have free reign, and free reign gives our emotions the liberty to make decisions on our behalf. Please keep in mind all the valuable information that we have learned up to this point. As a brief review, when we respond with our emotions instead of responding logically, we run the risk of violation. Therein lies the overarching problem because hurt people hurt people, and that is a perpetuation of dysfunction.

Since the Bible teaches us that love covers a multitude of faults (1 Pet. 4:8), we dare not dispute the legitimacy of the Word of God.

Instead, let's explore the need to love from a safe distance, because it is past time to stop the cycle of abuse. Repeat after me: "If your circle is toxic, it's time to become a square."

A square is a dated term for a prude, meaning that you are a killjoy, boring, dull, etc., and, in some cases, you are one who isolates themselves from the crowd. And isolating ourselves from toxicity and "bad friends" is exactly what I am challenging us to do here. Yep, you got it. Let's shout "PTL" from across the sanctuary, sis.

A few chapters ago, I challenged you to take inventory of your friends/relationships, and it's here that we will really begin to analyze the dynamics of each relationship individually. Now, before we begin, remember this is not social media. So haphazardly deleting, unfollowing, and blocking real life relationships based on an emotional whim is quite different from Facebook. In reality, dismissing our friends without due cause can have a lifelong impact as it can leave us alone and emotionally bankrupt. So, let's begin by dissecting the Word of God and gaining some insight about how the Bible portrays friendships.

Friendships are beautifully complex and they require love, longsuffering, selflessness, and trust. If you are rude, demanding, inpatient, and selfish, I wouldn't imagine that you have very many friends. Or the "friends" that you do have probably go out of their way to avoid you.

The most beautiful depiction of friendship is in the book of John 5:12–15, which reads:

> This is my commandment, that you love one another as I have loved you. Greater love has no one than this that someone lay down his life for his friends. You are my friends if you do what I command you. No longer do I call you servants, for the servant does not know what his master is doing; but I have called you friends, for all that I have heard from my Father I have made known to you.

This was John speaking about the crucifixion of Jesus Christ when he was preparing to die for the redemption of man. Let's face it, not many people are willing to accept the penalty for someone else's misdeeds. But this is how the Bible defines friendship. When we examine the well-known friendship between David and Jonathan, a beautiful story of brotherly love unfolds.

David and Jonathan are well-known for their close friendship. First Samuel 18:1–5 talks about the knitting of the two men's souls. Jonathan gave his robe and armor to David, essentially honoring David above himself and stripping himself of his kingly position (Jonathan's father was King Saul). Later, Jonathan stood up for David to his father (1 Sam. 19:1–7). Jonathan risked his life for his friend (1 Sam. 20). God used the friendship to preserve David for the throne. David, too, had deep loyalty to Jonathan. Second Samuel 1:17–27 is David's lament over the death of Saul and Jonathan. Even though Saul had been an enemy to David, the new king sought out someone from Saul's family that he might show him kindness for the sake of Jonathan (2 Sam. 9:1–13; 21:7). David's sense of loyalty to Jonathan and his gratefulness for their friendship outweighed the enmity between Saul and David. Here, the Bible gives us an award-winning recipe for the perfect friendship, including how to overlook flaws and cover one another. True friends "stick closer than a brother" (Prov. 18:24) and are edifying, encouraging, and sharpen one another "as iron sharpens iron" (Prov. 27:17).

The pastor of my childhood had a saying, "Telephone, telegram, tell a woman." Although sexist, I still find it comical and—as far as I am concerned—true since women have higher propensity to spread gossip in a much more fluid manner than our male counterparts. Since we have a knack for gossip, let's give it a go here. Our trusty notebook will be our listening ears and has been sworn to secrecy. That being said, you may want to either lock this notebook in a safety deposit box or set it ablaze once we're done.

Begin to document the last time that you had a disagreement with someone close to you. Be certain that you do not leave out any of the juicy details or substantiating evidence. Yes, sisters, let's get the skinny on the who, what, when, why, and the where.

- Who _____
- What

_____
_____
_____
_____

- When _____
- Why

_____
_____
_____
_____

- Where _____

Now that we have had the opportunity to write it all out, let's explore when it becomes necessary to address the issue with someone. To do so, we should consider a few key elements.

1. What relationship did I have with the person who I was in conflict with?
    a. Friend
    b. Coworker
    c. Family
    d. Stranger
2. How did the conflict affect me?
    a. Emotionally
    b. Spiritually
    c. Physically

3. What were the pros and cons of addressing this issue?
    Here is a helpful tool to guide you.
    Conflict Resolution Model (SAMSHA)
    a. Identify the problem
    b. Identify the feeling associated with the problem
    c. Identify the impact that the problem is causing
    Along with a few more steps that I added:
    a. Decide whether to run or resolve
    b. Talk about it. (Whether you decide to run or resolve,
        it deserves a conversation and, finally, sorry, ladies. No
        more hiding from issues. We are growing!
    c. Set boundaries. Boundaries have to be set in order to
        maintain both sanity and safety.

Boundary violations among friends cause conflict and may even
lead to the dissolution of an otherwise healthy relationship. Conflict
causes fatigue, and fatigue may cause us to behave in a manner that
is outside of our character. A former pastor once told me, "If it wasn't
inside of you, then it would not have come out." True, but even steel
wears out. There is only so much a person can tolerate before big
brother a.k.a. the beast is released. The idea then is to protect yourself
and others by demonstrating healthy boundaries.

Whether it's utilizing your personal power and saying no or by
clearly defining or redefining your boundaries, we must resist putting
ourselves in a position where we fall prey to chronic fatigue. Be honest about your pet peeves rather than dismissing them.

Considering everything that you have learned thus far, identify
one healthy way to tell a friend or loved one that you are bothered
by something that he or she is doing. Also consider your dominate
communication style and, if it's anything other than assertive, begin
to switch things up first. Closely examine your history of behaviors.

• Are you a yeller?—aggressive
• Do you tantrum?—passive aggressive

- Do you remain quiet and just take it?—passive
- Do you speak up about it in a calm, firm, and fair manner?—assertive

Review the ways that you have established boundaries in your friendships. What was effective versus what was not? To manage friendships effectively, we must be:

- Aware
- Reflective
- Insightful
- Honest
- Assertive

Being aware of our own personal needs, boundaries, idiosyncratic ways, and what we are willing or able to devote to a relationship is a basic component of a healthy relationship. So is being honest with ourselves by asking ourselves how other people view us. Sure, I think I am amazing, but how do the masses perceive me?

Self-reflection is a daunting task, as it requires us to be brutally honest with ourselves. With the birth of social media came the popularity of selfies. And trust me, prior to uploading the perfect photo, a grueling critique of yourself had to take place. If you have never taken a "selfie," consider your history of critiquing photos of yourself. Points to consider:

a. Retakes
b. Finding the best light
c. Avoiding the camera
d. Points of critique
e. Displaying your good side

Once you are done, document how your life might be different if selfies were taken of the inside, and you are now faced with the task of exploring and analyzing your behaviors, attitudes, treatment of others, etc., with the same level of intensity. Would you be your friend? With this concept in mind, we should outline attributes that we appreciate in a relationship as well as things that we are not willing to tolerate.

Which of your friends' attributes do you find desirable and which attributes do you find despicable? List at least four attributes that you are looking for in a friendship. List four things that you despise.

As you pay careful attention to both the desirable and the despicable characteristics noted above, consider how you feel when these qualities begin to manifest in a friendship. What qualities bring out the best and worst in you? Why?

Table 5. Examining Friendships Activity

Desirable	Despicable

Friendships require reciprocity; otherwise, it is not a friendship at all. One major complaint among women in my practice, both young and older, is misinterpreting a relationship. It is not uncommon to believe that you are in a friendship with someone who does not view the relationship the same way as you. This can be very hurtful for those of us who misinterpret the relationship and very awkward for the other person.

Here are few different types of friendly, nonbiological relationships that I would like us to consider.

Mentorship. This relationship derives from the second chapter of Titus when the older, seasoned women were commissioned to minister to and train the younger women. Mentorship should not be confused with friendship. It is more consistent with an internship where an intern or student trains under the tutelage of a skilled professional. Although pleasantries may be shared in a friendly and nurturing manner, the basis for the relationship is one of training.

Spiritual mothers. Spiritual mothers are similar to our natural or biological mothers and have been designated to assist in the spiritual maturation and matriculation of a younger, maturing woman in Christ. The dynamics of this role are defined by the hierarchical system. A mother is responsible for teaching and training the spiritual daughter. The lines become blurred, however, if the spiritual mother is spiritually or emotionally immature and become too familiar or casual with her spiritual daughter. I strongly caution spiritual mothers from sharing intimate details regarding her life and marriage unless it is intended for the purpose of training. In the case of training, self-disclosure is appropriate. Otherwise, confiding in her spiritual daughter or seeking advice or support taints the relationship. This leads to confusion in the relationship, diminishes trust, or, may cause the daughter to believe that there is a mutual, peer relationship or friendship. This can be especially damaging and hurtful to the spiritual daughter in the instance that boundaries become ill-defined. As a result, she is no longer invited to a social function or no longer privy to intimate conversations intended for a friend.

Big sisters. Big sisters in the Lord are seasoned, slightly older women who may not be old enough to be a spiritual mother but are too advanced in age and experience to be a peer. They possess the wisdom necessary to have a role in your spiritual development. Big sisters are role models who exemplify the conduct of a healthy Christian woman. These spiritual siblings may share intimate details with one another. However, certain details should be withheld from the younger sister out of respect of the relationship as well as to maintain the integrity and position of the big sister.

When I was in my teenage years, I had an older adult woman with whom my mother allowed us to spend time with. Initially, things were great, and she displayed the characteristics of a saved young woman, but then things took a turn. She had a spiritual setback and made no efforts to shield us from her sordid affairs. She shared intimate details about her sexual relationships and due to my immaturity in Christ and her influence in my life, I began to idealize her lifestyle. Although I knew that fornication was wrong, I romanticized the idea.

Sisters in the Lord (friends). Tried and true friendships that stand the test of time. These are most often peers of comparable age and experience. You are considerate of one another and are able to pick up each other's slack. True friendship is about the willingness to give and take without keeping score.

I have a few very close friendships. And boy have we fought over the years! From silly spats over a mutual crush in high school to snitching to each other's parents when we put ourselves in harm's way to actual physical contact. Yes, D, I am calling you out. And no, I am not changing any names. So, I welcome you to sue me, and we will split it two ways! I will gladly pay out, because this story is too funny not to give you all the credit that you are due.

So of course, she has amnesia, but we are about thirteen years old when she slapped me in church. Only God knows why especially since she does not seem to recall the incident. But my bestie was having one of her bratty "PK" moments, and I was no doubt standing my ground and before I knew it, a swift stinger across the cheek! Her dad seemed more embarrassed than shocked. But I was livid. My first mind said, *Drag her skinny behind across the sanctuary*, but I loved her too much to fight her.

Okay, let me stop lying. My mother was near, and I was not about to get my tail beat for fighting the pastor's daughter in church. So what did I do instead? I plotted to pommel her with snowballs at the upcoming youth snow trip. But the plan was foiled by a discerning youth worker, LOL! That was over thirty years ago and, in our defense, we were kids, so our brains were still underdeveloped. Each year, around the time of our birthday, I share this story and each year, she denies it. I think this may be kind of like "keeping score," but we enjoy roasting one another especially as it relates to age, and it's all in good fun.

Since that time, we have not been abusive to each other, and we continue to share the burdens of one another despite her revisionist history. Not even blood could give us a stronger, deeper connection.

Ministry associates. Ministry associates are those who we may serve alongside. But outside of church events, there is little or no social interaction. We may not particularly enjoy each other in any fashion, but we share mutual respect on the basis of doing ministry together for the edifying of the kingdom.

Obviously, the lines get blurred from time to time, or we find ourselves wanting more than others are able or willing to offer us. This happens quite often actually. Misinterpreting a relationship can be quite hurtful. I have sat across from countless women sharing the same story detailing the pain and rejection that is associated with misinterpreting relationships. A significant percent of my female clients who attend counseling due to problems in their interpersonal relationships find that they have misinterpreted a friendship and were heartbroken when they learned that their mentor was not their friend. And guess what? It's perfectly acceptable and, quite frankly, necessary that we take the time to grieve this loss just as any other loss in life. Instead of trying to force a friendship, accept the relationship for what it is and begin to invest time in others that you have more in common with. You should also strive to make yourself available for genuine friendships.

Be careful that you do not begin to despise the person that you were hoping to have a different type of relationship with. And try not to take it personal. Failure to reciprocate your desires does not make the other a bad person. It just means that you may have less in common than you initially believed, the two of you may not be a good fit for each other and are probably unequally yoked. So let us stop demonizing others because they happen to know themselves enough to understand that you are not meant to be a part of their inner circle. Trust me, I have been on both sides of the coin. The one desiring more and the one wondering scratching my head in bewilderment. Asking myself, "How in the heck did we get here?"

It's funny how we believe that we would somehow outgrow the desire to be someone's friend. I use the term funny facetiously, of course, because there is nothing funny about feeling undesired. Feeling undesired is loss, even if others do not understand losing something that we never had possession of. But it's the loss of a dream. As we have envisioned our lives together, sharing triumphs and tragedies, funny stories about our kids, husbands, and careers.

Women need women. Well, let me speak for myself. I without a doubt or ounce of shame, need strong supportive women in my life.

I need women who are smarter, more studious, and more gifted than I am to stretch me, challenge me, and give me that desire to keep going, to keep dreaming. I also need women who are not as far along on life's journey as I am because it gives me the motivation to keep striving to show those who blaze the trail behind me that they can do it, too! A cup and pitcher, ladies. Iron sharpening iron. So yes, I need the applause, the "girl you got this!" the "Sis, you did that!" and the "Wow, how'd you do that?"

While others may choose to pretend that accolades are unnecessary, I take pleasure in the acknowledgment because I remember a time when I was invisible. Remaining cognizant of my origin as well as the countless tears and residual agony that paved this path, I know if it had not been for God on my side, I would have been consumed. No vain glory here. He deserves all the praise and when they ask me how, I say, "It was Jesus."

Humility is a friend of mine, and I desire nothing more than to return the gesture. Ladies, when we know that our sisters have our back and that she desires for us to be successful, life is just better.

Contrarily, when our sisters set traps and snares to entangle us, trip us up, or make us fall, it subtracts from us. And yes, whether we dare to be vulnerable enough to admit it, it hurts. For me, it's like the mean girls on the playground all over again or the pretty girl crew who denied me a seat next to them. Leaving me embarrassed, rejected, and fighting tears that I prayed no one noticed.

Foes: Haters and Dream Killers

If I've said it once, I've said it one thousand times—please do not engage in a battle of wits with your haters a.k.a. dream killers. It's a waste of breath and resources that can be used to sow into your purpose. Fighting is exhausting especially when it's a never-ending, uphill battle. Once you fight off one hater, another pops up in its place. It's kind of like when you pluck weeds—you can completely rototill and lay concrete, but if there is even a sliver of earth remaining, a weed finds a way to persevere and pop through the cement. Just like a hater.

If you ask me, haters or dream killers are a necessary component for our success. Let's just consider it resistance training. Here's my theory:

1. Our haters are a conduit for change. For one, we may not know what's in us until our haters call it out. When someone looks to discredit us, it may sound like this, "She struts around here trying to be *all perfect*, tsk, and that PhD has gone to her head. I know she has a degree, but it doesn't take all that." Second, when someone is hyper-focused on our failure, that's all the more reason to be successful. Sis, don't even try to pretend that you don't take pleasure in proving your haters wrong. It's a true *but God* moment!
2. Our haters are supporters in disguise. When they see something valuable about what we have to offer, "the spirit of Cain" emerges. Jealousy and envy are vicious.
3. Your haters may highlight your mistake but remember that your mistakes have equipped you for the journey ahead, so never waste the pain.
4. Pain is a part of the process.

And remember, "Learn to use criticism as fuel, and you will never run out of energy" (Woodward).

Balancing Life, Love, and Ministry

Sisters, I simply could not write about living our best life in Christ without addressing one of our most pivotal roles, that of a wife. In fact, one could argue that it was the very reason for our creation—for man's good pleasure. Ladies, we were created to solve the problem of man. Woman was created intentionally, not just on purpose, but with purpose.

> And the Lord God caused a deep sleep to fall upon Adam, and he slept: and he took one of his ribs, and closed up the flesh instead thereof; And the rib, which the Lord God had taken from man, made he a woman, and brought her unto the man. And Adam said, This is now bone of my bones, and flesh of my flesh: she shall be called Woman, because she was taken out of Man. Therefore shall a man leave his father and his mother, and shall cleave unto his wife: and they shall be one flesh. And they were both naked, the man and his wife, and were not ashamed. (Gen. 2:21–25)

Please take a few moments to relish in the fact that we are God's gift to man and humanity. And the very next time anyone asks you who you think you are. With confidence and enthusiasm declare, "God's gift to the world!" I hope this makes you smile as much as it makes me smile. For when purpose is pumping through our DNA, we should exude a certain level of *God-fidence*, which is that inner glow and radiance that only comes from a confidence given by our creator. For we are "fearfully and wonderfully made. "Wonderful" are his "works" and "my soul knows it very well" (Ps. 139:14). Meaning, there is no need to doubt our excellence, our splendor, nor the works of his mighty hand. Downtrodden for what? Our Father uniquely crafted us to minister to one man in a way that no other can. So why would we ever despise our calling to be a helpmeet?

Is it even possible to be angered by or have wrath toward a man we were created to assist? Before we go there, I first want to make a bold statement; one that I believe may free someone one who is riddled with guilt or is despising her current call and season in life. Even though woman was created to be a helpmeet and life companion for Adam, God uses women regardless of marital status.

Single is not a dirty word, divorce does not mean desperate, and becoming a widow is not your death sentence. Do I need to say this again, have you touch your neighbor for the third time, or put it in a hymn? Certainly, most women desire to be married, at least that's the word on the streets and certainly the common plight of the women that I serve in my therapy practice who feel incomplete and impotent if no one has bothered to put a ring on it. And I absolutely must say this. Any ol' man is *not* better than being alone.

Trust me when I say, while some of us are praying for our Boaz, countless other women are praying some son of sedition off them and out of their lives. In more severely damaged marriages, some women found infidelity to be the much-needed break they had been looking for, as it awards them the liberty to finally walk away. Others have learned that finding the ego strength to finally say good-bye to abusive relationships in general outweighed the fear and anxiety that they once had of being alone.

For the next several pages, we will walk through the Word of God and take a glance at how God used many different women, regardless of age, culture, marital status, or socioeconomic class. This is important because many women hold the misconception that they have no purpose outside of marriage and that perception would easily anger anyone.

Let's begin with Sarai whose name was changed to Sarah.

Sarai. Sarai is commonly known as the "Mother of Nations" and at other times has been referred to as the "Mother of faith." Sarai was ninety years old and her husband (*baby daddy*) was a hundred years old when they conceived her only child, Isaac. Could you imagine bearing your first child at that age? This was no doubt miraculous, so much so that when the man of God initially prophesied that she would conceive, Sarai laughed. Honestly, some of us would have laughed and mocked the man of God, too. Think about it, the Bible says that she and her husband Abraham were "well stricken in years" (Gen. 21:1). That is code for *dried up*, because she was decades past menopause. So, there was absolutely no way humanly possible for her and her hundred-year-old husband to conceive.

Can someone say, "But God!" The Lord certainly has a way to make us laugh. Genesis 21:6 reads, "And Sarah said, God has made laughter for me; everyone who hears will laugh over me."

I could only imagine the thought of God saying, "Oh, you don't believe I can impregnate a seventy-year-old woman? Let me go ahead and add twenty-five years on it." As the promise did not come into fruition until twenty-five years later.

See, Sarai, like many of us, doubted God and decided that she would speed along the process by giving Abraham her handmaid to carry out the promise. If you read the story, that didn't work out very well for anyone involved. In fact, this fiasco led to the continuous war between the two half brothers. But God came back to Abraham saying, "Abraham, as for Sarai thy wife, thou shalt not call her name Sarai, but Sarah shall her name be. And I will bless her and give thee a son also of her: yea, I will bless her, and she shall be a mother of nations; kings of people shall be of her" (Gen. 17:15–17). Once she allowed God to have his way, she bore a son Isaac, the grandfather of Jacob, whose name was later changed to Israel, of the infamous "children of Israel."

You think you are too old and faithless to be used by God? Nonsense. #FaithRestored!

Okay, I hear some of you saying… But I'm not old, and she was married. Touché. So, let's take a look at Mary, the mother of Jesus.

Mary. Mary was still a virtuous, virgin, teenaged girl when she was overshadowed by the Holy Ghost and used as the vessel to bring salvation into a dying world. I'm sure you remember the story, but I will bore you with a few of the details regardless. She was engaged to be married to Joseph, and they had never had any sexual contact. No outercourse, foreplay, or physical intimacy of any kind. So there was absolutely no chance that he could have impregnated her. Once she began to show signs of pregnancy and it could not be concealed, he pondered how he could break off the engagement privately since during this time, women were put to death if they became pregnant out of wedlock. This was especially heinous since Joseph, her intended husband, was not the father. But the Angel of God came to him and let him in on the secret.

Matthew 1:18–25 tells us:

> This is how the birth of Jesus the Messiah came about[a]: His mother Mary was pledged to be married to Joseph, but before they came

together, she was found to be pregnant through the Holy Spirit. Because Joseph her husband was faithful to the law, and yet[b] did not want to expose her to public disgrace, he had in mind to divorce her quietly. But after he had considered this, an angel of the Lord appeared to him in a dream and said, "Joseph son of David, do not be afraid to take Mary home as your wife, because what is conceived in her is from the Holy Spirit. She will give birth to a son, and you are to give him the name Jesus, [c] because he will save his people from their sins. "All this took place to ful-fill what the Lord had said through the prophet: "The virgin will conceive and give birth to a son, and they will call him Immanuel" [d] (which means "God with us"). When Joseph woke up, he did what the angel of the Lord had commanded him and took Mary home as his wife. But he did not consummate their marriage until she gave birth to a son. And he gave him the name Jesus.

So there you have it, an example of a teenager used by God and for such a powerful role! Wow!

Now, I'm hearing the skeptics say, but my past is sketchy. I'm certainly not virtuous, and my virginity...well, let's not even talk about that. Okay then. I have one for that, too. Let's talk about Rahab, shall we?

Rahab. Rahab was a "harlot," which is an antiquated term for prostitute. But the Lord still saw fit to use her for his glory. Joshua 6:25 explains, "And Joshua saved Rahab the harlot alive, and her father's household, and all that she had; and she dwelleth in Israel even unto this day; because she hid the messengers, which Joshua sent to spy out Jericho." Before you say, "So what! She hid spies. Sounds like she should be arrested, not awarded." Let me give you a history lesson. Remember the story about the wall of Jericho and how the children of Israel marched around the wall for six days and on the seventh day, they gave a great shout and the wall fell flat? Some of us were probably too busy shouting and running around the church to truly understand the significance of this. But Rahab was actually being used by God, and this was a part of her redemptive process.

The spies that she hid were of Israeli descent, and overtaking Jericho was essential in order to enter into Canaan, the land that was promised to their forefathers. Rahab bartered and advocated for the salvation of her family in return for hiding the spies in her home. She eventually won the heart of Prince Salmon whose father was an Israelite leader. She later bore Boaz, the husband of Ruth. And we *all* know that story, right?

"The Book of Hebrews enrolls Rahab among the faithful along with Sarah. These are the only two women mentioned by name in the famous roll call of the faithful" (Wine, 39). So she's kind of a big deal! Too scandalous? I think not, nothing is too scandalous for God!

I think I may have your attention now. As you can see, God continues to use women in mighty ways and in various roles. Let's continue.

Deborah. Deborah was a wife, a prophetess, and a judge who led an entire nation She was the "only woman in the Bible who was placed at the height of political power by the common consent of the people" (Jacobs). Originally, Deborah was merely the wife of an "obscure" man, but her purpose began to evolve as her faith in God increased. She was a visionary, a counselor, and a warrior. It's truly an amazing story and if you are in need of some real life "Girl Power" inspiration, I pray you find the time to read it.

While I know all of us are not fiery, spirited warriors, and we do not all have the capacity to lead a nation, we are all called to do something great. That leads us to Naomi, who was a humble, heartbroken widow who lost her husband and both of her sons.

Naomi. Naomi was the widowed mother-in-law to Ruth and was actually the person who introduced Ruth to the one and only true God as Ruth was from a heathen nation. And as the story goes, Ruth later married Boaz, the son of the former harlot Rahab, and begat Obed, father of Jesse, and grandfather of King David, the father of Solomon, who built the temple and is known as the wisest man who ever lived. All are in the line of Christ.

Of course, I cannot stop there.

Esther. a young girl from the wrong side of the tracks, was, for all intents and purposes, considered a "reject" because of her lineage. How many of us feel like outcasts at times? I certainly have my days when I feel like I don't measure up. Sure she was young and beautiful, but so were the other virgins who were also anticipating their one night with the king. I'm sure she had to fight the fear and rejection of not being worthy enough to be desired by the king, especially since her people were forced into slavery. We now understand that she was "called for such a time as this" to save an entire nation of people. This was after she won the heart, favor, respect, and, ultimately, the crown of a powerful man, and wed the Prince of Persia. This was certainly an instance of "it doesn't matter where you've been, it's where you're going." And Esther went all the way to the top.

To continue in this fashion is really quite boastful. But I do enjoy bragging on our Savior. So, here's the story of Eve—The Mother of Humanity.

Eve. We all know the story of Eve, but I think we lose sight of the fact that God used her despite her major mistake! Like the destruction of humanity. Adam called her the mother of all living things, even after the fall of man. "And Adam called his wife's name Eve; because she was the mother of all living" (Gen. 3:20). So please spare us all the bitter, pity party and resist saying, "I've been too bad, you don't know what I've done..." Look at what she did! And the Lord used her, regardless.

I went through this entire mini history to demonstrate that we have purpose and ministry in us. And no matter our season in life—married, single, divorced, or in the midst of scandal—God has given us worth and that means that we must work. Even when we don't feel up to it.

When we are idle for too long, we become restless and irritable, which is a sign that you should be active in ministry. We must find something for our hands to do, something that serves someone other than ourselves, something that demonstrates the true essence and love of God. A question that I am often asked is, "How do I know what my ministry is?" and I always point them back to God. But not before giving them a few practical pointers to get the wheels turning.

1. What do you enjoy doing?
2. In what areas do you believe you are naturally gifted?
3. What is one function in the church that tends to bring you the most joy or put a smile on your face?

I suggest that you start there, along with meeting with your pastor, First Lady, or designated leader. They can be pretty good at helping members to navigate through the challenging task of getting involved in ministry. And don't be afraid to try your hand at a couple of different things until you find your niche. I do caution people to start out slowly and gradually work your way up to major roles. That way, if it doesn't work for you, you won't appear to be indecisive or unreliable. And if it doesn't work for the ministry, the letdown for you may not be as painful. Besides the servitude, being involved in ministry also has other benefits such as:

1. Combatting boredom
2. Maintaining accountability
3. Character building
4. Resume building
5. It's a great way to meet other like-minded individuals (and who knows, maybe even your Boaz)
6. Can keep us out of trouble by having something of value to take part in

For those of us who are married or have children, we have a bit more—okay, we have a *lot* more ministry to do. If we are not careful, our roles may become a burden and begin to breed anger when we do not have the proper resources. This is a good time to touch on single parenting for a moment.

I was married, living single for almost seven years while my ex-husband chased his next high and whatever women who were too damaged to disapprove of his disgraceful lifestyle. And although it was difficult, and I hated him, not once did I despise motherhood. That's only because by the time my daughter was born, I had already taken my place at the feet of my savior and rejected the misnomer that I was "both the mother and the father." I hear women say this, and while I understand the premise, it is biologically incorrect, not biblically sound and actually makes things more difficult when women choose to adopt this idea.

To all my single ladies, the Lord cares for you, too. Here is an example of how the Lord made provision for a fatherless child and his mother.

> Then the word of the LORD came to Elijah: "Get up and go to Zarephath of Sidon, and stay there. Behold, I have commanded a widow there to provide for you." So Elijah got up and went to Zarephath. When he arrived at the city gate, there was a widow gathering sticks. Elijah called to her and said, "Please bring me a little water in a cup, so that I may drink." And as she was going to get it, he called to her and said, "Please bring me a piece of bread." But she replied, "As surely as the LORD your God lives, I have no bread—only a handful of flour in a jar and a little oil in a jug. Look, I am gathering a couple of sticks to take home and prepare a meal for myself and my son, so that we may eat it and die." "Do not be afraid," Elijah said to her. "Go and do as you have said. But first make me a small cake of bread from what you have and bring it out to me. Afterward, make some for yourself and your son, for this is what the LORD God of Israel says: 'The jar of flour will not be exhausted and the jug of oil will not run dry until the day the LORD sends rain on the face of the earth.'" So she went and did according to the word of Elijah, and the woman, Elijah, and her household had food to eat every

day. The jar of flour was not exhausted and the jug of oil did not run dry, according to the word the LORD had spoken through Elijah. Later, the son of the woman who owned the house became ill, and his sickness grew severe, until no breath remained in him. "O man of God," said the woman to Elijah, "what have you done to me? Have you come to remind me of my iniquity and cause the death of my son?" But Elijah said to her, "Give me your son." So he took him from her arms, carried him to the upper room where he was staying, and laid him on his own bed. Then he cried out to the LORD, "O LORD my God, have You also brought tragedy on this widow who has opened her home to me by causing her son to die?" Then he stretched himself out over the child three times and cried out to the LORD, "O LORD my God, please let this boy's life return to him!" And the LORD listened to the voice of Elijah, and the child's life returned to him, and he lived. Then Elijah took the child, brought him down from the upper room into the house, and gave him to his mother. "Look, your son is alive," Elijah declared. Then the woman said to Elijah, "Now I know that you are a man of God and that the word of the LORD from your mouth is truth." (1 Kings 17:8–24)

Sisters, I truly hope that you read the passage and challenged yourself to avoid falling prey to the statistic that Christians do not read our Word as discussed earlier in this guide. If you skimmed, or skipped it altogether, please take a few minutes to go back and read it, especially if you are single parenting or you happen to love someone who is. Because it outlines a story of faith and putting our trust in God. It exemplifies the heart of the Father who sends the man of God to care for a single parent and her fatherless son.

Another example of God's provision can be found in the New Testament:

> Therefore I tell you, do not be anxious about your life, what you will eat, or what you will drink, nor about your body, what you will put on. Is not life more than food, and the body more than clothing? Look at the birds of the air: they neither sow nor reap nor gather into barns, and yet your heavenly Father feeds them. Are you not of more value than they? And which of you by being anxious can add a single hour to his span of life? And why are you anxious about clothing? Consider the lilies of the field, how they grow: they neither toil nor spin, yet I tell you, even Solomon in all his glory was not arrayed like one of these. But if God so clothes the grass of the field, which today is alive and tomorrow is thrown into the oven, will he not much more clothe you, O you of little faith? Therefore do not be anxious, saying, "What shall we eat?" or "What shall we drink?" or "What shall we wear?" For the Gentiles seek after all these things, and your heavenly Father knows that you need them all. But seek first the kingdom of God and his righteousness, and all these things will be added to you. "Therefore do not be anxious about tomorrow, for tomorrow will be anxious for itself. Sufficient for the day is its own trouble (Matt. 6:25–34).

Ministry isn't always easy, but it is always rewarding, if not on earth, then certainly in heaven. Ministry is our charitable, contribution of love defined by our actions. I was a single parent for seven years before the Lord saw fit to gift me and baby girl to Tobaise. During that seven-year sabbatical, the Lord was increasing my faith in him as my Savior, my Lord, and my continued consultant. I was a busy mama who worked full time. I was a full-time student and kept my hand to the plow in ministry. Because I had suffered so much loss and had the high propensity to fall prey to vain self-reliance, I had to stay connected to ministry. It was my lifeline.

I established and faithfully led a 5:00 a.m. intercessory prayer ministry. Monday through Friday, whether there was rain or bitter California cold, regardless of holiday or me praying alone, my children and I were there. It was there, in ministry that God allowed me to catch the attention of my forever husband Tobaise. I wasn't searching for a husband, nor was I looking to be found. In fact, I'd had my fill of men and was hiding out, tucked under the shadow of the Almighty. So Tobaise had to go through God to find me.

Sisters, it was finally time for my purpose to become clear. A prophetess had told me a few years earlier, "Your marriage is your ministry, and your ministry is your marriage." I didn't understand what she meant because I was single and *not* even looking to mingle. But God had other plans and was preparing me just as he prepared Esther in the Book of Esther, and he was "bringing me before great men" (Prov. 18:16) so that he would be glorified.

This leads me back to our original role. Woman was created to be a helpmeet for her man, and when man and woman come together, the woman multiplies. Sisters, our family just as the Lord designed, is still our first ministry. Now, that does not mean to forsake the things of God. For everything is funneled through our relationship with him. "If anyone comes to me and does not hate father and mother, wife and children, brothers and sisters—yes, even their own life—such a person cannot be my disciple" (Luke 14:26). It is important to note that hate, in this context, simply means to love less, not despise, or have contempt for.

Speaking of despise, sometimes, we despise our calling to our husband, too, if we are not cared for properly. Before I speak on this, let's first talk about the essence of love. There are several types of love that I want to explore—Eros, Ludas, Philia, Storge, Agape, and Pragma. Here is an excerpt from Psychology Today.

Eros

Eros is sexual or passionate love and is the type most akin to our modern construct of romantic love. Eros is filled with romantic, sexual desire.

Ludus

Ludus is playful or uncommitted love. It can involve activities such as teasing and dancing, or more overt flirting, seducing, and conjugating. The focus is on fun, and sometimes also on conquest, with no strings attached. *Ludus* relationships are casual, undemanding, and uncomplicated but, for all that, can be very long-lasting. *Ludus* works best when both parties are mature and self-sufficient. Problems arise when one party mistakes *ludus* for *eros*,.

So, first of all, uncomplicated? Really? The entire definition of Ludus appears complicated. Remember I told you earlier that there are no such things as emotionless sex or unattached sex. How can you have sex with a man and expect there to be no strings? What about the one that is lassoed around your heart, tethered to your emotions, and attached to your high reactive behaviors? No strings? That is clearly a secular school of thought. Nonetheless, let's continue with the excerpt.

Philia

The hallmark of *philia*, or friendship, is shared goodwill. Aristotle believed that a person could bear goodwill to another for one of three reasons: that he is useful; that he is pleasant; and, above all, that he is good; that is, rational and virtuous. Friendships founded on goodness are associated not only with mutual benefit but also with companionship, dependability, and trust.

Plato, the best kind of friendship is that which lovers have for each other. It is a *philia* born out of *eros*, and that, in turn, feeds back into *eros* to strengthen and develop it, transforming it from a lust for possession into a shared desire for a higher level of understanding of the self, the other, and the world. In short, *philia* transforms *eros* from a lust for possession into an impulse for philosophy. Real friends seek together to live truer, fuller lives by relating to each other authentically and teaching each other about the limitations of their beliefs and the defects in their character, which are a far greater source of error than mere rational confusion: they are, in effect, each other's therapist—and in that much it helps to find a friend with some degree of openness, articulacy, and insight, in order to be changed.

Storge

Storge ('store-gae'), or familial love, is a kind of *philia* pertaining to the love between parents and their children. It differs from most *philia* in that it tends, especially with younger children, to be unilateral or asymmetrical. More broadly, *storge* is the fondness born out of familiarity or dependency and, unlike *eros* or *philia*, does not hang on our personal qualities. People in the early stages of a romantic relationship often expect unconditional *storge*, but find only the need and dependency of *eros*, and, if they are lucky, the maturity and fertility of *philia*. Given enough time, *eros* tends to mutate into *storge*.

Agape

Agape is universal love, such as the love for strangers, nature, or God. Unlike *storge*, it does not depend on affiliation or familiarity. Also called charity by Christian thinkers, *agape* can be said to encompass the modern concept of altruism, defined as unselfish concern for the welfare of others. Recent studies link altruism with a number of benefits. In the short term, altruism leaves us with a euphoric feeling—the so-called 'helper's high'. In the longer term, it is associated with better mental and physical health, as well as longevity. At a social level, altruism serves as a signal of cooperative intentions, and also of resource availability and so of mating or partnering potential. It also opens up a debt account, encouraging beneficiaries to reciprocate with gifts and favors that may be of much greater value to us than those with which we feel able to part. More generally, altruism, or *agape*, helps to build and maintain the psychological, social, and, indeed, environmental fabric that shields, sustains, and enriches us. Given the increasing anger and division in our society, and the state of our planet, we could all do with quite a bit more *agape*.

Pragma

Pragma is a kind of practical love founded on reason or duty and one's longer-term interests. Sexual attraction takes a back seat in favor of personal qualities and compatibilities, shared goals, and making it work. In the days of arranged marriages, *pragma* must have been very common. Although unfashionable, it remains widespread, most visibly in certain high-profile celebrity and political pairings. Many relationships that start off as *eros* or *ludus* end up as various combinations of *storge* and *pragma*. *Pragma* may seem opposed to *ludus*, but the two can co-exist, with the one providing a counterpoint to the other. In the best of cases, the partners in the *pragma* relationship agree to turn a blind eye—or even a sympathetic eye, as in the case of Simone de Beauvoir and Jean-Paul Sartre, or Vita Sackville-West and Harold Nicholson.

Loving Tobaise made me question everything that I thought I knew about love and the magic that happens when God joins two people together. Knowing what I do now about the various types of love, my abuser may have, in fact, been sincere when he said, "I love you." This makes it possible for someone to have a form of love for you such as Ludas, yet never fulfill you emotionally like the other more compassionate, selfless types of love. With this thought in mind, perhaps it's Ludas mistaken for Eros that leads to a woman despising her role.

Other reasons may also include:

1. Misuse of power, including be subjected to:
   - infidelity
   - abuse
   - neglect or withholding affection which is considered emotional abuse
2. Ineffective communication
3. Immaturity—marrying prematurely before you are emotionally and/or spiritually capable
4. Marrying outside of God—marrying a nonbeliever
5. Lack of balance in your life—when all of your time is spent with your husband, with no outside interests or life, or purpose outside of your husband.

I don't have to tell any of us, that women sometimes marry without consideration for our future by making a lifelong commitment to someone who is not suited for us. I hate to believe it, but I do think that many women got caught in the trap of "it's better to marry than to burn" and end up marrying for the sake of physical pleasures and one's inability to maintain self-control rather than marrying for the desire to commit and minister to our husbands. Again, if it's not you, it's definitely someone that you know. And to be honest, you probably wish that you didn't know them because you are likely getting sucked into an emotional abyss and swallowed up by the incessant conversation of how she is leaving her marriage, yet again. There is virtually nothing worse than feeling stuck in an abusive marriage that you can't get yourself out of.

One of the lowest points in my life, and the only time I wished to never wake up, was when I was married to a man who didn't have the capacity to love me the way I desired to be loved. He didn't love God and he certainly didn't love himself, based on the amount of cocaine that he snorted on the regular and the crack that he free-based at the risk of losing it all—his family included.

I didn't even realize how depressed that I was until my MD began to ask probing questions about the fingerprint-shaped marks that were on my knee. I hadn't even realized that they were there as I had gotten dressed in anticipation of meeting with my physician that day. And because I didn't believe that it was a big deal, I didn't feel the need to lie when I shared that things had gotten a bit physical the night before.

I mean I had been thrown around and even hit by his car in the past, so him restraining me and forcing me to perform sexual favors didn't seem much like abuse. I mean, we were married after all, right? It wasn't until my doctor said, "You deserve to be treated like a lady," that I realized things were really bad. A few moments later, a female social worker sat next to me and asked, "If you could go anywhere, where would you go, and who would you take with you?" My answer was, "Some place far with me and my babies." Geesh, was that a cry for help? This novice therapist didn't realize that she was being psychoanalyzed. Learning about the various types of love seriously had me questioning, "What is love and what in the world does love have to do with anything?"

When I first met Tobaise, dating him was the furthest thing from my mind. And I get this question all the time. "Really? But he's so handsome!" as they give me that condescending, "Yea right!" side eye. But when I tell you I was so totally head over heels in love with Jesus, that I was totally oblivious to everyone. Sure he was handsome. But so were the other dudes I married before. So, if I were making a list of what I wanted in a marriage—which I was not—handsome wasn't even a determining factor. When a woman has endured the hell that I subjected myself to by marrying outside of God and to a "nonpracticing" but heavily entrenched Muslim man. Trust me when I say, solitude is golden, and I couldn't care less about handsome. True love that only comes from Jesus is all that a girl truly needs in a husband and once God has the heart of a man, the rest of him will follow.

"What God had joined together, let no man put asunder" King James certainly had a way with words. In layman terms, when God joins two people together, no one should be able to pull them apart. But the question is, how do we know it was God's doing?

Ladies, if I had the answer for this, I would not be on my third marriage. Thankfully, I have certainly grown since the immature age of nineteen when I first married, and I have grown even more since the second time that I said, "I do," when I was twenty-nine. Though I suppose that some may judge me by the number of marriages alone, you miss the beauty in all this. The beauty that I could not even fathom until about ten years ago. God was developing me. Like the amazing Father and teacher that he is, he used every mistake and all the pain that it entailed to fuel my purpose. Only God can do that.

So now when I ask myself, "Nett, what makes this relationship different?" or when people wonder what gives me, a two-time divorcee, the credibility to counsel others in their marriage? I point to the degrees lined across my wall and point a single finger up to Jesus. He was my savior before, but now he's my Lord. And this time, I did something that I'd never done before. I invited him to my wedding.

5

Kingdom Sisters Speak

W omen are amazing. Each one of us has been uniquely designed, and our own intrinsic personality, mannerism, foibles, and assets have been downloaded into us by our creator. Although no two women are the same, we share more similarities than we do differences. I invited all of my social media followers to share their anger story and ten eager women responded.

I interviewed eight women from different age brackets, ethnicities, socioeconomic backgrounds, and Christian denominations. I asked eight women the same seventeen questions, and their responses have been documented in their own words. Their names have been changed to protect their privacy. However, other information has been used with their permission.

As you read the next several pages, I invite you to continue to take notes, as you pay close attention to common themes that these women share. Some said more, others said less, but I pray that their story of resilience and reliance on God blesses you as much as it did me.

Interviews

Layla

Layla was a forty-three-year-old African American woman. She had been married for two years; however, her husband is currently incarcerated. Layla had two biological children from a previous relationship and three additional foster children of whom she had been the legal guardian for eight and a half years.

1. *When did you first realize that anger was a problem in your life?*

   I realized that anger was a problem in my life by the time I was eighteen years old.

2. *How has anger affected your life?*

   Anger has caused me a tremendous amount of internal emotional and physical distress. I have anxiety and depression. I experience nightmares often and have panic attacks. I only have one friend who is not a relative because she is the only one who knows how to interact with me. My husband and I almost divorced during our first year of marriage. I also take antidepressants, antianxiety medication, and sleep aids. All of this is not due to my anger alone, but anger is definitely part of the problem.

3. *Who do you believe was impacted the most by your anger?*

   My adult children are angry all the time. It seems to me that they have a lack of happiness. I notice that my oldest daughter does not find any enjoyment in life. I believe she has taken on a lot of my negativity on life. Also, she has heard me express the anger I have toward some family members. And even though I can still interact with them, she cannot because of the negative things I have said.

   My young adopted children are constantly trying to please me so that I stay in a good mood. My eight-year-old constantly says sorry and that he loves me. He has told his teacher that no one likes him and that he wants to kill himself.

4. *How does anger impact your varying relationships, children, romantic relationships, brothers and sisters in Christ, etc.?*

I don't believe I have any friendships with the brothers and sisters in my church. People avoid me, except for my mother, aunt, uncle, and cousin. I've had some heated conversation with a few church members and now they hug me and move on quickly. My children are afraid of me and are constantly trying to keep me happy. My husband and I are better now, but we would have explosive arguments. The word divorce was coming out of my mouth almost every week, if not daily. I have very few coworker friends. I don't interact with anyone outside of work except my adult daughter or my sister. My sister and I just recently reconnected.

5. *If anger was not a problem in your life, how might things be different?*

I believe that if anger was not a part of my life, I would not have as many health problems. I would be able to enjoy my life more and have a closer spiritual relationship with God, family and friends.

6. *Do you believe that it is okay to be angry?*

I believe there are times when it is good to be angry but not to stay angry. Anger can motivate someone to change their life for the better or fight against an injustice.

7. *What do you believe is the root of your anger?*

The root of my anger is my parents. My mom constantly told me all the horrible things my father did to her and what he didn't do for our family, but she expected me to love and respect him. The things my father did or didn't do were true. I had to beg for his help as a child and adult. Most of the time, I was cussed out and told no. My mom could not or would not help me out at times. She would badger me into going to my dad for help. My mom did everything and still does for her sons, but the daughters have to fend for themselves.

160

I hate her for not protecting me from sexual abuse. For bringing strange people into our home who mistreated me and stole from me. I was forced to give up my bedroom for these random drug addicts. My father also neglected to protect me both physically, emotionally, and financially. He yelled every time he spoke, and my mom excused it as "that's just how he is." When someone yells at me or just speaks firmly, I go into panic mode. I usually shut down and cry. This makes receiving feedback at work or school painful for me. My mom would say horrible things about church members then expect me to hug and smile in their face. She had no problems doing it. I find myself overly confronting people because it seems my mother keeps her head buried in the sand. I vowed to never let anyone hurt me again, to protect my own children at all cost and not put up with other people.

8. *What was the worst thing that has happened as a result of your anger?*

The worst thing that happened to me as a result of my anger is a lifetime of depression and anxiety. The anger has sucked the life out of me. Although things are better now, I cannot regain the time I lost.

9. *How long did anger govern (have control over) your life? If currently struggling explain.*

Anger had practically complete control over my life from age eight to thirty years old. I was molested at the age of eight and twelve by the same person, who my mom welcomed into our home both times. She did this even after knowing that I had been abused. Her response was, "Let's see if it happens again." I literally cussed at her when I was in my twenties about that statement. I regret speaking to her that way and would never do that again. After years of self-destructive behaviors, at age thirty, I started going to therapy. I hesitated to go to therapy out of shame. I believed that if I was a real Christian, then prayer should have been enough to solve all my problems. I now take antidepressants and antianxiety pills that have also helped with my anger. I walk and meditate. I even take herbal supplements to help.

10. *What has been helpful in dealing with your anger?*

Prayer (which I rarely do), exercise (which is hard to keep consistent), medication, extra rest, focusing on projects (volunteering), and talk therapy. Reading which I love to do, positive self-talk, positive posters, and spiritual YouTube videos. I acknowledge my anger, seek to find the root of it and how I can change things. My mantra is, accept what I can't change, change what I can and ask the Lord to show me the difference between the two.

11. *What has not been helpful for you?*

Focusing on my anger or seeking revenge. Not acknowledging my anger and allowing it to fester inside me. Skipping my praying, exercising or medication and therapy appointments. Smoking cigarettes and overeating. Trying to please people all the time and doing activities to avoid facing the real issues. Overspending.

12. *How do you respond to anger?*

Depending on who I am angry with, I respond many different ways. I lash out at my mom. I yell at the young children. I stop speaking to my oldest children and my husband. I get defensive with outsiders (coworker, church people, and strangers). I have a very hurtful tongue that I have practiced over the years, saying the most hurtful things I can say as a retort. Many times, I will prepare hurtful statements in advance, or for a just in case moment and definitely for the next time moments.

13. *Do you talk to God about your anger? If not, why? If so, how often?*

I used to pray twice a day, every day until I got pregnant out of wedlock *again* (eleven years ago). I felt like my pastor was saying I was worthless to him, God, and the church. I was crushed and now I rarely pray. I might pray once a week but even then, I have serious doubt if Jesus wanted to hear from me.

14. *How often does your anger manifest?*

My anger manifests every day. Usually with my youngest son or my mom. My youngest struggles with behavior problems in school and talks incessantly. I get to the point where I tell him to just shut up. My mom likes to beat around the bush and manipulate and play the victim. If I don't confront her directly, I tell my oldest daughter how I am feeling. I will get all worked up then go smoke.

15. *Is your anger ever misunderstood, if so how?*

I believe my anger is often misunderstood. My anger is a sign of me hurting. It's also my defense mechanism to protect my inner child and my own children.

16. *Have you ever been incarcerated due to your anger?*

I have never been incarcerated for any reason. Although I could have if the police were called. I have pulled knives on people, set things on fire, and bleached my ex's clothes inside his apartment.

17. *Have you ever hurt yourself or others due to anger?*

I believe smoking is hurting me. I have taken more pills than I should to fall asleep. I overspend. I overeat. I have engaged in risky sexual behaviors. But I have never attempted suicide or cut myself. I have considered suicide, but hell is real. I have overdisciplined the children. I have yelled at them and said hurtful things that I later regret. I do apologize, but I cannot take the words back. I avoid making new friends and isolate myself.

Spit Fire

Spit Fire was a fifty-six-year-old Puerto Rican/French and Irish woman. She was divorced with a total of seven children. Five of her children were adults. Two of her children were her eight and nine-year-old grandchildren that she had adopted and was raising as her own.

1. *When did you first realize that anger was a problem in your life?*

   It was Christmas 2018... I was extremely grumpy and miserable. I became extremely confrontational with my son, and I saw the fear in his eyes. It made me cry that I scared him and allowed myself to get so angry that I could have hurt him. There was *no* reason for me to be so angry.

2. *How has anger affected your life?*

   I start to break things. I don't want to be around people, I become judgmental and negative.

3. *Who do you believe was impacted the most by your anger?*

   My family, I took everything out on them.

4. *How does anger impact your varying relationships, children, romantic relationships, brothers and sisters in Christ, etc.?*

   I didn't want to be around people.

5. *If anger was not a problem in your life, how might things be different?*

   I'd be happier, not so lonely

6. *Do you believe that it is okay to be angry?*

   Yes, it's okay to be angry; however, the way it's handled is crucial.

7. *What do you believe is the root of your anger?*

   Trust. Fear of not being good enough and being disrespected.

8. *What was the worst thing that has happened as a result of your anger?*

   Seeing my son afraid of me; he wasn't himself.

9. *How long did anger govern (have control over) your life? If currently struggling explain.*

For over one year.

10. *What has been helpful in dealing with your anger?*

Setting boundaries, knowing that it's okay to be angry, talking to myself and my Father (Jesus) following through with consequences. When I tell my kids that there is a certain consequence for an action, I make sure to follow through, so things don't begin to build up.

11. *What has not been helpful for you?*

Different methods work on different situations... sometimes, I give myself a time-out... I relive the situation in my head so I can calm down....at that moment, when I realize it, I talk out loud to myself. It seems I always ask myself the same question first, why did it make you angry? That causes me to really examine myself. Once I realize why I became angry, it helps me handle the situation better and look at the situation differently. Sometimes, I can just breathe and calm down. So to me, everything has been helpful either alone or in combination, mostly in combination.

12. *How do you respond to anger?*

I take time out to process...ask myself why did it make me angry? And I try to understand the other person's heart.

13. *Do you talk to God about your anger? If not, why? If so, how often?*

Yes. From the moment I wake up 'till I lay my head to rest, all day, I'm learning to do life together with him.

14. *How often does your anger manifest?*

I lost my temper one time in the past two months. When I'd given a specific set of instructions and they are repeated to me (so I know that they understand), but the child does everything opposite. When asked why they say, "I don't know," that totally makes my blood boil. Since taking the anger management class, I have learned not to take it personally. I've learned that he is different from my other children and that he is a requires a one-on-one, side-by-side, work together kind of kid.

15. *Is your anger ever misunderstood, if so how?*

Oh yes! Well me, myself, I didn't even understand it. I'm now learning the difference and that myself alone am responsible for my response. This helps me.

16. *Have you ever been incarcerated due to your anger?*

Never.

17. *Have you ever hurt yourself or others due to anger?*

Yes, when I was younger. I broke someone's jaw, because they wouldn't shut up. I tried to kill myself in 1992 and as a result, spent nine months in a psychiatric hospital. I've handled things as best as I could until the church I attend for over fourteen years closed. I tried being strong but noticed I was getting angrier and not talking to my Father (Jesus). One day, after blowing up on my son, I saw the look in his eyes. I cried and asked the Father for help because I didn't want to go down that old road again. Soon after that, you popped up on my Instagram page. I don't even know how; we are on opposite sides of the country. I believe it was divine connection. Daddy brought us together, and I am eternally grateful! Soul sisters!

Denise

Denise was a thirty-four-year-old African American woman. She was married with one child.

1. *When did you first realize that anger was a problem in your life?*

   When I was faced with two charges of aggravated assault with a deadly weapon.

2. *How has anger affected your life?*

   Anger has made me more aware and unapologetic in how I treat myself and others.

3. *Who do you believe was impacted the most by your anger?*

   Me, I am the one who suffered the most because of my anger.

4. *How does anger impact your varying relationships, children, romantic relationships, brothers and sisters in Christ, etc.?*

   It doesn't anymore. It used to create issues with how open I would allow myself to be. Most of my triggers were people. So, I would distance myself from a person in an instant!

5. *If anger was not a problem in your life, how might things be different?*

   I would be further along in my personal journey. My financial, mental, and emotional health would be better and more stable.

6. *Do you believe that it is okay to be angry?*

   Yes, anger is okay.

7. *What do you believe is the root of your anger?*

   The root of my anger was mainly because I was accustomed to a certain structure and lifestyle. So people who challenged that didn't live up to my standards had the nerve to feel entitled or tell me that I was being unreasonable in my standards, it struck my worse nerve.

8. *What was the worst thing that has happened as a result of your anger?*

    Nothing really bad has happened to me, others have suffered.

9. *How long did anger govern (have control over) your life? If currently struggling explain.*

    Roughly five years of my life. It doesn't overcome my life anymore though.

10. *What has been helpful in dealing with your anger?*

    What helps me most to deal with my anger is really, enjoying my freedom, hot water, the feeling only a man can give me. I do not appreciate being in closed, confined quarters with women (jail).

11. *What has not been helpful for you?*

    It doesn't help that I have become more passive. That's when my aggression builds, and that can be problematic.

12. *How do you respond to anger?*

    Initially, I process, analyze, and sometimes laugh. Later, I regroup and respond in the way that best serves me.

13. *Do you talk to God about your anger? If not, why? If so, how often?*

    Nah, I don't tell God about my anger. No particular reason why not. I don't hold it to an esteem to be bothered as much as I used to be, so there isn't a need to discuss it.

14. *How often does your anger manifest?*

    My anger manifests in actions, no matter how lethal. Words, no matter how hurtful, and emotional, no matter how damaging. So, I try to keep anger away as much as possible. The "click out" is *real!*

15. *Is your anger ever misunderstood, if so how?*

    Nah, my anger is understood. It's resoundingly known. No confusion as to the level or intent of my anger. It's almost effortless when I am provoked.

16. *Have you ever been incarcerated due to your anger?*

Yes, I have been incarcerated because of my anger. So, let's begin by explaining why I had these charges in the first place. It was a time in my life where being single and savage was my reality. I was not sanctified, but I was perpetrating a saved lifestyle. I was dating several guys at once. I asked, or should I say, required one of them to complete a task. After a few days of it not getting done, I contacted someone else to help me out. So the first guy was all in his ego [feelings]. The first guy (who I initially asked to help me) and his son were both visiting and staying in my home at the time, so I paid to house them in a hotel while the other guy completed the task. While I thought it was very mature of me to even get him a hotel, he was butt hurt and, in his ego, (feelings). I really couldn't have cared less...#savage.

Well, upon leaving the hotel, after dropping them off, this guy decides that I shouldn't leave them there. Unbeknownst to me, he proceeds to insert his son into my car window as I am driving off! Crazy right! The kid ends up falling and bystanders who witnessed the ordeal called the police and reported that I ran them both over with my car.

SMH. So the question that you asked earlier, what was the worst things that has happened to me as a result of my anger. My answer is nothing. If you ask was I angry due to the situation. Yes, afterwards...I was pissed!

For two years I couldn't get a decent job because my background check showed that I had been charged, not convicted for two potential *felonies* that I didn't even commit!

17. *Have you ever hurt yourself or others due to anger?*

Yes, I have hurt others, and in doing so I've hurt myself.

Brown Sugar

Brown Sugar was a fifty-five-year-old African American woman. She was a three-time divorcee with two adult children.

1. *When did you first realize that anger was a problem in your life?*

   May 1983.

2. *How has anger affected your life?*

   It led me to a life of addiction.

3. *Who do you believe was impacted the most by your anger?*

   I would say that I was the most impacted by my anger, yes, my parents endured some things, but I was the one that really carried that heavy load of anger, which took me from one level of anger to another level. To a level that makes you feel like you don't belong nor fit in the world that you are in. You just live day after day not trusting nor believing anyone truly cares for you.

4. *How does anger impact your varying relationships, children, romantic relationships, brothers and sisters in Christ, etc.?*

   I didn't want to be around people. I isolated myself, I didn't have women friends. The mental institution took a toll on me, and I didn't want to be around them. I didn't know how to really socialize until the Lord got a hold of me. The Lord allowed me to be mad at him. He understood my position. I didn't even talk to him before the day that he spoke to me for the first time. He was my mother's and grandmother's God.

   I ended up in a Christian-based, drug treatment program in 2008, and my life changed. It was after watching the *Passion of the Christ* that I was able to forgive my mother.

   My daughter was very young, but what impacted them was my drug addiction, they really didn't know what I had been through, 'cause I never revealed it. When I spoke at a women's service recently, which was the first time my daughter really heard what happened to me. Now that they know what drove me to the drugs, they understand, but just wish I had chosen a better way to deal with my anger. But they felt my pain, too. They always prayed for me, I never allow them to see my pain, I am or was good at covering up, so they wouldn't have to live like that.

5. *If anger was not a problem in your life, how might things be different?*

Wow, my life could have probably been a life without hate, shame, embarrassment, very low self-esteem. A better relationship with my mom, so many years of hate and anger with her. I know I missed some years of mother and daughter time. Also, I might not have felt that my kids deserved a mom who was better than me.

6. *Do you believe that it is okay to be angry?*

Yes.

7. *What do you believe is the root of your anger?*

When I was wrongfully institutionalized in a mental institution. It was after I heard a voice tell me, "Don't you go!" It was when I was about to leave with my date to get some white stockings to go with my outfit. We were headed to go party. He was going to go and pick them up for me, but I felt that he would take too long, so I was getting ready to ride with him. When I got ready to open the door to leave the house, I heard the voice say, "Don't you go." I was like, "What was that?" It was as loud and clear as you and I are talking now. So, I didn't go. Later, he came back to the house, and he was bleeding from his head. Me and my friend ran outside and saw people standing around the ditch, a ways down the road. When we ran down there, we saw the car in the ditch and became hysterical. I then knew it was the voice of the Lord telling me not to get in that car. But no one believed me, and they ended up taking me to the hospital to get checked out because I wouldn't calm down.

My family and the doctors said that I was hallucinating, and that God does not speak to people like that. My mother was given the option to let me walk away from the hospital or institutionalize me and she had me institutionalized. I received electric shock treatment, and I hated her for that.

I also saw my father jumping on my mother and since she never called the police, I thought it was okay. So I found myself in an abusive relationship, too. I felt stuck, and it became a revolving cycle.

I didn't have anger before then. I had it going on! I was in high school when I had a daughter. I had a track scholarship and was on track to go to college. My life changed drastically; it was all shattered in one night.

8. *What was the worst thing that has happened as a result of your anger?*

Drug addiction, I took my anger out on everyone, I was angry with mom and then the Lord revealed to me that I had a "malice spirit."

9. *How long did anger govern (have control over) your life? If currently struggling explain.*

Twenty-three years.

10. *What has been helpful in dealing with your anger?*

A drug addiction program. I was holding unforgiveness, pointing fingers, and blaming others. But God delivered me from people and also what others would think about me after God was through with me. He delivered me from people before he delivered me from my addiction.

11. *What has not been helpful for you?*

Turning to crack cocaine to try and numb my anger and hurt has not been helpful. Being alone also has not been helpful. Loneliness sometimes causes me to feel angered, but God has had me in a season of celibacy for the past four years. So whenever I start to feel lonely, God starts to fill my schedule. I am in several ministries at church, including altar worker, and in the choir. So I am at church as often as I can, when the doors open, I try to be there.

12. *How do you respond to anger?*

     I really don't fool with anger anymore. I don't let any-
thing get that close to me, to get me upset these days. And
when I am upset, I don't act out like that anymore. So if
I'm upset, you won't know it. My thing now is trying to
find a way to fix it, to make it all right even if it's not my
fault. God has groomed me to be the peacemaker.

13. *Do you talk to God about your anger? If not, why? If so, how
    often?*

     God revealed things to me. As I began to
read about others in the Bible who also witnessed
the voice of the Lord and how they had people
who did not believe them. The Lord gave this
scripture to me, "blessed is the man that is per-
secuted for righteousness sake, for theirs is the
kingdom of heaven." Because I heard him audibly
and then saw the car in the ditch after he spoke to
me, my mind could not be changed. No amount
of electric shocks could erase that from me.

14. *How often does your anger manifest?*

     Like I said, not much today. Don't let the sun go
down on your wrath and I don't ever, *ever* want to be in a
place like that again.

15. *Is your anger ever misunderstood, if so how?*

     Yes, I misunderstood my own anger, I now under-
stand that I wasn't angry. I was embarrassed, ashamed, felt
unworthy, frustrated and hopeless with no future. I was
suicidal, I attempted suicide two to three times by taking
pills. Someone found me, and I ended up getting my stomach pumped. But I'm still here!

16. *Have you ever been incarcerated due to your anger?*
     No.

17. *Have you ever hurt yourself or others due to anger?*

     Yes, I attempted suicide two to three times in the past.
I never thought my story would be important enough to
put in a book. But I am happy to share and to help others.

Laverne

Laverne was a forty-two-year-old African American woman. She was a divorcee with two adult children.

1. *When did you first realize that anger was a problem in your life?*
   Twenty-four.
2. *How has anger affected your life?*
   In the past I would fight, hit people, black out, I have also gotten arrested.
3. *Who do you believe was impacted the most by your anger?*
   My children.
4. *How does anger impact your varying relationships, children, romantic relationships, brothers and sisters in Christ?*
   It has been passed down to my children.
5. *If anger was not a problem in your life, how might things be different?*
   My relationship status may be different. I probably wouldn't have angry children.
6. *Is it okay to be angry?*
   To a certain extent, if it is kept under control.
7. *What do you believe is the root of your anger?*
   Unsure.
8. *What was the worst thing that has happened as a result of your anger?*
   Getting arrested.
9. *How long did anger govern (have control over) your life? If currently struggling explain.*
   A long time. I couldn't control my words or my temper.
10. *What has been helpful in dealing with your anger?*
    Repentance.
11. *What has not been helpful for you?*
    N/A.

12. *How do you respond to anger?*

    I now ignore situations that will allow me to act outside of my character.

13. *Do you talk to God about your anger? If not, why? If so, how often?*

    Yes, in prayer daily. Anger is no longer an issue for me.

14. *How often does your anger manifest?*

    Before I was able to manage my anger, daily.

15. *Is your anger ever misunderstood, if so how?*

    Yes. It would sometimes be thought as sadness.

16. *Have you ever been incarcerated due to your anger?*

    Yes. Once I was pulled over for speeding. Whenever I deal with anger, I have a high level of anxiety. So that night, when I was pulled over by the police, I continuously overtalked them. I did not adhere to their warning to stop resisting and stop being argumentative. I became more argumentative and ended up being arrested.

    Another time, I was drinking heavily and someone made me mad. I took off my shoe and begin to beat her in the head with my stiletto heel. I believe she received stiches. There was certainly bleeding.

17. *Have you ever hurt yourself or others due to anger?*

    Yes.

Delphina

Delphina was a fifty-six-year-old African American woman who was engaged to be married at the time of the interview. She did not disclose if she had any children.

1. *When did you first realize that anger was a problem in your life?*

   Early in my teens, although I wasn't sure what it was at the time. I was in therapy which helped me to gain a better understanding.

2. *How has anger affected your life?*

   It has driven me to succeed or attempt to succeed in all that I do. On the other hand, it has been debilitating due to my "hair-pin anger" trigger. I react first before responding. It has gotten in the way of proper communication and understanding. It's my defense mechanism. It causes me to push someone out, watch how they respond, and then attempt to draw them back in. I have spent the majority of my life having the need to protect myself; whether it was my own perception or a real need. So my anger was both good and bad.

3. *Who do you believe was impacted the most by your anger?*

   My family was impacted the most. It caused me to not be able to hear. I don't believe they were aware of the cause of my anger, so if they hit me wrong on one of those days, it was all bad!

4. *How does anger impact your varying relationships, children, romantic relationships, brothers and sisters in Christ, etc.?*

   It has certainly minimized them. Since being redeemed, it's been a complete transformation. Recently, they have only seen bursts of my anger. In the past, people were very afraid, and they had every right to be because I was very volatile. I was intentionally abusive because I thought I could do that. I have not been able to make amends with some of them, so I don't see them anymore.

But I wasn't just popping off for the sake of popping off. It was legitimate. Recently, my fiancé experienced the other side, the flip side of me. Although it was warranted, my response was excessive and now we both must remember that this person is still there. Being the closest person to me, my fiancé gets the blow out, even when not the blame.

5. *If anger was not a problem in your life, how might things be different?*

Anger and my past made me who I am today. Gives me the tools and the passion that I have to minister.

6. *Do you believe that it is okay to be angry?*

Yes, anger is valid.

7. *What do you believe is the root of your anger?*

Molestation. Also, one of my parents was an alcoholic. So, watching how my father responded to anger and not having a voice to talk about the molestation, the anger began to fester. Fear is a root, fear of abandonment, fear of being abused, fear of rejection and losing.

To be able to say this, I know that I have grown.

I am not afraid as an individual. There are degrees and even not knowing something also makes me angry.

8. *What was the worst thing that has happened as a result of your anger?*

It was the worst and the best but becoming incarcerated. Not knowing the system or understanding and recognizing my anger extended my time. The mental illness that happens to an individual, that happens to victims of molestation…which led me to abuse myself for twenty-eight years on crack.

9. *How long did anger govern (have control over) your life? If currently struggling explain.*

I'm not currently struggling, other than confessing that the daily drama and conflama that this country is subjecting us to. But I'm not even sure that is considered anger at this point, because it becomes laughable. But about twenty-eight years while I was on crack.

10. *What has been helpful in dealing with your anger?*

Jesus! If it had not been...kinda thing. Working for God without looking for a return. He invested in me, so I owe it. I attend worship service each week whenever I am not traveling and preaching or attending Bedside Baptist.

11. *What has not been helpful for you?*

People telling me that I should not be angry.

12. *How do you respond to anger?*

My vehement comes in my words. But my face looks angry all the time, even when I am not. So others believe I am angry when I am not. If I were at a ten, I would be red and menacing loud.

13. *Do you talk to God about your anger? If not, why? If so, how often?*

Daily, sometimes I laugh at God because he created me this way. I ask him what he was thinking to have me around people who he knows anger me. I trust God and he trusts me to know me.

14. *How often does your anger manifest?*

Not often anymore. My body can't take it anymore. It takes life from me so it's a due diligence to work on it on a daily basis. I intentionally have few friends that helps to salvage my nerves... I know me. Because the stupidity and ignorance of others is a trigger.

People can't help who they are. They have foibles that annoy me. I have a choice to either be angry or try to be loving as best as I can. But due to the state of the world, I am constantly angry. Some days, I get angry because I have to be better than my anger. When I began to listen to the voices in my head and let it fester, brew, or go ignored, the voices in my own head tell me that I am stupid for letting something go past.

15. *Is your anger ever misunderstood, if so how?*

Yes. I am a very protective individual, so I get very passionate about the people that I love so my body naturally responds. People tell me to calm down, but I'm not mad. I don't like injustice and people think I'm mad, but I'm only pontificating about a truth as I see it.

Even when I am not mad people think that I am because I don't smile a lot or walk around cheesing. I'm also a deep thinker so my forehead is always crunched up. People try to fix me, but this is how I respond.

16. *Have you ever been incarcerated due to your anger?*
    Yes.

17. *Have you ever hurt yourself or others due to anger?*
    No, not physically. But yes, by damaging people that considered me a friend and people that I love. I go hard now because I didn't go hard back then, now I'm like get out of my way! Me trying to erect a boundary seems like abuse to others. But I attempt to be whole and healthy for us all.

Isabella

Isabella was a fifty-four-year-old Latina/Native American woman. She was married with four adult children. Isabella attended weekly worship services including Bible studies whenever her health permitted.

1. *When did you first realize that anger was a problem in your life?*

   In my early to midtwenties. I was blacking out and was later told that I was doing things out of character. I would pick up a knife or another weapon and go after someone.

2. *How has anger affected your life?*

   I was impacted quite a bit, pushing people away, not trusting people. In the early years, I thrived on revenge. I would rather hurt them before they had a chance to hurt me.

3. *Who do you believe was impacted the most by your anger?*

   Anybody close to me; children, siblings, friends, relationships.

4. *How does anger impact your varying relationships, children, romantic relationships, brothers and sisters in Christ?*

   With my children, for one, I passed down my anger to them and for two, it really put a wedge in there. It took a lot of years to rebuild the damage that I put on them.

   My romantic relationships in the past, there were a lot of relationships that I just could not keep. I just could not keep one. I was too angry, and I took things out on them whether it was their fault or not. A lot of these anger issues that were manifesting were way before my life with Christ. I was a hot mess before him. Now, when I do get angry, it's a little bit easier to identify why I'm actually angry and not take things too personally. I then begin to talk to Jesus.

5. *If anger was not a problem in your life, how might things be different?*

   Oh, wow! I would have healthier relationships and I don't think I would have so many life issues, you know?

6. *Is it okay to be angry?*

I think at times it is, it just depends on what you do when you are angry that makes a big difference. For me, when I was angry, I didn't know what to do with the anger so I would start lashing out verbally or physically. And back then, I was a major alcoholic and drug addict, so I just didn't care. And when you mix any of those together, it was just explosive. I just wanted to start fighting.

7. *What do you believe is the root of your anger?*

I know a lot of it stemmed from my childhood when I started drinking; and once I started drinking, it all started surfacing. A lot of people got hurt, then came the shame and embarrassment that I tried to cover up. A lot of it started from child molestation and not being heard, no action was taken. When I should have been protected, I wasn't. The person that I did tell was my mother. And because it was her brother who violated me in the back seat of a car when I was just a little girl…I remember that my head would barely touch the roof of the inside of the car.

I blocked it out for a lot of years. It started to resurface in my teenage years when a lot of other stuff started coming out. Growing up in an age where you are to be seen and not heard, you just hold it in, and it starts building up and you start self-inflicting wounds and stuff.

8. *What was the worst thing that has happened as a result of your anger?*

There are quite a few. I became a cutter, suicidal, trying to hurt other people who started hurting me. So it's kinda hard to pinpoint.

9. *How long did anger govern (have control over) your life? If currently struggling explain.*

It's not as bad now, but over the last so many years, it has resurfaced again. It's when I forget or fail to realize that I have not given it over to the Lord. I have to tell myself, "Girl this isn't your problem." A lot of it stems from my marriage and a lot that is going on in my marriage today.

I have a habit of stuffing down my feelings, and things are starting to be pushed down again. I want to talk about it and put things out in the open, but my husband just wants to shut it down.

10. *What has been helpful in dealing with your anger?*

Oh, wow! I think lately I have to try to come up with healthy self-care to kind of release. When things get out of control, I tend to become a shopaholic. I don't buy things for me. I spend money on others. I will justify it by saying, "Oh, well, he shouldn't have made me mad." But recently, I started buying plants instead to focus on something healthy.

I put on my praise and worship and refocus and regroup. I talk to the Lord and remind myself that I am about to be in jail or something, and I don't want to go that route. I don't want to be that same ugly, broken person anymore.

11. *What has not been helpful for you?*

Stuffing it.

12. *How do you respond to anger?*

I go to exploding, no filter…then I completely shut down. I start crying and pushing everyone away. For me, that's a danger zone.

13. *Do you talk to God about your anger? If not, why? If so, how often?*

I do and depending on how bad it is or how many episodes. I feel that conviction. What I have been doing lately is asking God to help me while in the moment. I ask him to help me to forgive and to deal with it in a better way, and it has helped. Other times, I just want to be mad at that person. But now, I laugh at God, "Like you ain't even right," because I want to stay mad at that person and I can't.

14. *How often does your anger manifest?*

It happens less and less. It takes a whole lot to even get me to that point. But before, it was several times per week. But as far as getting to a nine out of ten maybe once or twice a year.

15. *Is your anger ever misunderstood, if so how?*

Yes. I learned that anger is just a symptom because something is going on underneath. I think for me, it's when I'm not being heard or respected. Whenever I feel that my feelings or views are being minimized.

16. *Have you ever been incarcerated due to your anger?*

Yes. LOL! I can laugh now. But a lot of times, it began with me popping off at the mouth. One time specifically, we were all drinking. I was with my mom. I was nowhere near being saved. My mom was kidnapped and the person that I was dating knew the people who kidnapped her, so I wanted to go find her. But he was too high to even talk. She eventually escaped and ended up at a park where she began to explain that two or three guys tried to rape her.

I was still trying to get my date to tell me where the other guys were and when he didn't, I started beating him up in front of the cops, so I went to jail.

17. *Have you ever hurt yourself or others due to anger?*

I would get angry and start fights. Mainly directed toward males, and I didn't care if I got whooped on. That's the way things were handled in our family, we fought. You get violent and talk later. As a kid, we got a lot of whoopins and I didn't know any better, so I did the same with my children. I get mad and get to spouting off at the mouth, start cussing at the kids and then get the belt.

There were other times as well. Okay, this gets a little dark in my late teens through my early twenties when I was married to my first husband, I was going to kill him. I was planning to chop his body up and feed him to my pigs and put his bones in a barrel of acid. There was constant abuse, physical, sexual, emotional, and blackmail throughout the years. There were multiple trips to the ER and many broken bones. I was even held prisoner in my own home. He made threats, that if I left him, he would take my kids and leave the country.

Another time in my mid to late twenties after my divorce, my daughter was molested by someone I was dating. I was working with the police to trap him; he was connected to the mafia. I end up getting kidnapped and held hostage for over twenty-four hours (which was not a part of the plan) I managed to escape, but it affected my anger significantly. I dug deeper into drugs and drinking and had such rage that I didn't even recognize myself anymore.

I had friends who were a hitman who wanted to put a contract out on him, but for some reason, I just could not go through with it. But we both know why now. It was God.

There is so much more but that's just a little sliver of my anger.

I hope this helps someone. And I do not mind you using my real name because all of this is under the blood. And by the grace of God, I'm still alive to talk about it.

Marie

Marie was a forty-six-year-old African American woman. She was a two-time divorcee and had two adult children.

1. *When did you first realize that anger was a problem in your life?*

When I was about twelve years old, I was asking my mother about my biological father. She told me that I didn't need to know who he was and to basically get over it. I have a different father than my siblings, who had a father in their life. I remember screaming at the top of my lungs and pulling at her. I remember being so angry that she had to restrain me. It was very personal for me. I couldn't understand why she would do that to me, why she would keep me away from my father and not answer any questions about him. I was always the quiet one. So this was very different for me.

But I really noticed that my anger was out of control, when my son who was seven years old at the time was taken by CPS and I ended up taking anger management classes. I am able to look back at myself like "wow," it's so crazy. He was holding my face in his hands and saying, "Mommy, please, I just want to sleep with you." He was crying and asking to lay down with me. His brother had just left for Louisiana to be with his father, and he did not want to sleep in his room alone. But I had my boyfriend in my bed, and it wasn't even an option.

He kept coming back and forth into my room asking to lay with me. He was crying, and I didn't even try to console him. I didn't try to read to him or any other method. I just whooped him. I took him back into his room and started whoopin him. He had welts all over his body. That negative moment was a defining moment for me. I needed to learn to pull back due to the losses that I had, but I had no filter. That was fourteen years ago.

2. *How has anger affected your life?*

I've pushed people away, but it's made me a better person. I have certificates to prove it.

3. *Who do you believe was impacted the most by your anger?*

My son.

4. *How does anger impact your varying relationships, children, romantic relationships, brothers and sisters in Christ?*

I honestly think I have distanced myself in times when I felt upset. In my romantic relationships, I actually wasn't as angry as I should have been. I just allowed the abuse, I allowed the cheating until it just piled up, and then I started lashing out, throwing things.

5. *If anger was not a problem in your life, how might things be different?*

That's a good question. I think just looking at the incident with my son was an eye-opener for me. The funny thing about this question is that I don't want things to be different. I really needed to know this about me. Would I have been more in control or in hindsight a different person, I'm not sure. Looking back, I don't know how to answer that, but my son and I are best friends now. I really needed that. We can laugh about the situation now. Now I can talk to other women and pray with them about their anger.

6. *Is it okay to be angry?*

It's healthy to communicate it. To take time to think about my response.

7. *What do you believe is the root of your anger?*

Fear of being out of control. I didn't want to look like I didn't know what I was doing as a mom. I was overly concerned with what others would think of me. At work, at church. So, I had to pretend to be in control at all times. I always felt like I needed to square up. So for me, it was fear.

I learned from my mom. She was mostly the expressive one when she got angry. She yelled, cried, and she drank a lot. My stepdad would leave the house at times when he was really angry. He drank too, but I got the feeling early on that he didn't like arguing with my mom I actually felt sorry for him when she yelled at him.

8. *What was the worst thing that has happened as a result of your anger?*

Losing my son to CPS. The funny thing is, God spoke to me earlier that day before the incident and said, "This is going to hurt, but I will be with you." I was cooking at the time, so I thought he was talking about me being burned so I took my hand off the pot immediately. And later that day, the incident happened.

9. *How long did anger govern (have control over) your life? If currently struggling explain.*

Not much longer after that. I mean I had some incidents, but nothing as bad as that.

10. *What has been helpful in dealing with your anger?*

Talking about it, being honest about hurt feelings. Being open with my kids and telling them, wait, I need a minute or don't talk to me like that" I am better at communicating now. Talking about it helps. Talking to you helps, it's such a release to be able to talk about my father and things that have happened in my life.

The Holy Ghost. I let God just handle it. I can take a deep breath and hear scripture. Prayer, definitely prayer. I cry now because I see people differently from a different perspective. They get a lot more grace and mercy now. I know how to ask God to get this off of me 'cause I am feeling some kind of way

11. *What has not been helpful for you?*

Holding it in. Not telling people that it wasn't a good time to talk or not giving myself time to process something before I respond.

12. *How do you respond to anger?*

Throwing things, tearing people up with my words. I would let it pile up and then start pulling things out the freezer and throwing them at people. I was like a hurricane and then I would leave the house a mess for an entire day just so they could see what chaos looked like. Instead of saying, "You're cheating, I'm pissed!" I would just throw things… I never said it right then and there.

13. *Do you talk to God about your anger? If not why? If so, how often?*

Yes and I can talk to others about it now, too. People can benefit from the healed me, and we can go to the throne of grace together.

14. *How often does your anger manifest?*

I don't get upset like that anymore because I can talk to friends in real time or pray about it. LOL! I walk down the halls at work and say, "Lord! Get this off of me"

15. *Is your anger ever misunderstood, if so how?*

Yea, when I feel taken advantage of. The biggest thing is when I feel like I am being taken for a fool. A lie is disrespectful. When I am ready to talk about what I am feeling…I don't know how to define that emotion. But when people are talking to me like I'm stupid, then I'm like, "I can show you better than I can tell you," then I go off. But the one thing is when I feel like I have to defend myself.

16. *Have you ever been incarcerated due to your anger?*

No.

17. *Have you ever hurt yourself or others due to anger?*

Yes.

Wow, right? Each woman different, yet still the same in the sense that the anatomy of their anger all began with pain. Anger can be a beast, big brother settling a score. Or anger can be an ally once we learn to give our pain up and surrender it to the Lord.

I hope that you have come to realize that as women, we desperately need each other. So we must learn to all get along. We must find the beauty in celebrating the women who paved the path before us while we encourage the ones who trail behind. It's time to learn how to have each other's back instead of planning an ambush or plotting an attack.

Sisters, don't let the devil win by falling prey to the same old tricks and recycled lies. We are the daughters of Zion, and we represent the Most High!

The Emotional Benefits of Laughter

Life is but a vapor and can be tough as nails. So it's important that we take the time to find pleasure in the simple things, find joy in great company, and remember to always count our blessings. Proverbs 17:22 reads, "A joyful heart is good medicine, but a crushed spirit dries up the bones."

So why not laugh a little?

"Strength and dignity are her clothing, and she laughs at the time to come" (Prov. 31:25). Meaning, no matter the calamity, we got this, sis! And the Lord, "He will yet fill your mouth with laughter, and your lips with shouting" (Job 8:21). If we allow him to govern our lives.

"Then our mouth was filled with laughter, and our tongue with shouts of joy; then they said among the nations, "The LORD has done great things for them" (Ps. 126:2). You see, laughter is biblical.

Sisters, it's just about time to say good-bye. So here is our final activity. This can be done as an individual project first and with a group of friends later. This activity, as most of the activities listed in this manual, is lifted from the pages of the HolyGhost HomeGirls Handbook (Brookins).

Activity:

1. Select one of the scriptures about laughter and briefly explore it with your group.
6. Answer the following questions with your group:

When was the last time that you laughed out loud (LOL)?

What were you doing?

Who were you with?

How often do you laugh in general?

Who were your HomeGirls (longtime friends) growing up?

What kinds of activities did you engage in?

1. What did you learn about laughter during this exercise?

_____
_____
_____
_____
_____

7. What did you learn about yourself during this exercise?

_____
_____
_____
_____
_____

8. Which activity can you implement into your regular routine to combat boredom /apathy?

_____
_____

THE ANATOMY OF ANGER

_____

_____

_____

Sisters, the quality of our lives is based on the caliber of the company that we keep. First Corinthians 15:33 tells us, "Do not be misled: Bad company corrupts good character."

9. Name two to three Kingdom sisters (or others) that you can share one or more of these activities with?
    a. _____
    b. _____
    c. _____

Listen, ladies, as we wrap this thing up, I leave you with a simple charge to keep God first and let everything else fall into place. Never forget that we are more powerful than we think and more precious than we often realize. The burdens that we lug around like donkeys are better when surrendered to the Savior.

When we are filled with the precious gift of the Holy Ghost and succumb to his spirit, we have the power to tread upon serpents, and all that we truly need to live our best life in Christ is to resist the enemy and take sweet rest at the feet of Jesus.

Sweet Surrender

Tis so sweet to trust in Jesus,
Just to take Him at His Word
Just to rest upon His promise,
Just to know, "Thus saith the Lord!"
Jesus, Jesus, how I trust Him!
How I've proved Him o'er and o'er
Jesus, Jesus, precious Jesus!
Oh, for grace to trust Him more!
I'm so glad I learned to trust Him,

Precious Jesus, Savior, Friend
And I know that He is with me,
Will be with me to the end.
Oh, how sweet to trust in Jesus,
Just to trust His cleansing blood
And in simple faith to plunge me
'Neath the healing, cleansing flood!
Yes, 'tis sweet to trust in Jesus,
Just from sin and self to cease
Just from Jesus simply taking
Life and rest, and joy and peace.
Amen.

CONCLUSION

So my sisters, as I conclude this book, there are still many questions to be answered, and honestly, try as we may, and as brilliant as scholars and practitioners claim to be, no one has managed to unlock the secret to eliminating anger. Therefore, my theory regarding anger bears some weight. That is, anger itself is not the problem and is actually a vital component of our human lives. Instead, learning to manage anger opposed to censoring anger is the answer to the age-old question, "Why does anger run rampant in the church?"

Although potentially painful for my family and others involved, sharing these private events of my childhood and my early years in Christ has been liberating. You see, the Lord allows us to encounter and endure things in life so that we may be a blessing to the kingdom. And my prayer is that the heinous things that I am recovering from become things that you only read about.

I pray that you have learned that devotion to our Christian coping skills, healthy boundaries, regular self-care, and the reciprocal support of our HolyGhost HomeGirls, a.k.a. our Kingdom sisters, are not a luxury afforded to some. Rather, these are necessities when it comes to living our best life in Christ. The eight other sisters and I were brave enough to share our stories and did so honestly. Learning a new way to approach anger is no easy feat as big brother will stay checking for us, and he is simply doing his job. So, do yourself and those who love you a favor: when big brother comes knocking at your door, don't ignore him. Ask him what he needs and check in with yourself. Trust me, it makes a world of difference.

So, where do I go from here? Well, my journey is not complete. There are many books to be written on the topic of anger including being a self-bully, many workshops to teach, many sisters to encourage, and three beautiful daughters to lead, love, and support. My lifetime of dealing with anger and the insights that I have gained from sitting across from countless beautifully flawed women like you continues to drive me to research the anatomy of anger, to uncover the fear and pain, and to help women to find a voice and platform to safely express it. And while I am at it. I strive to debunk the stigma that relates to anger. Yes, saved women get angry. And rightfully so. Anger is unavoidable. But with Christ it is absolutely, without a doubt, manageable.

REFERENCES

"Abortion." *Science Daily*, 2019, https://www.sciencedaily.com/terms/abortion.htm. Accessed 3 May 2019.

Brookins, Antionette. *The HolyGhost HomeGirls Manual.* HolyGhost HomeGirls, 2017, https://www.holyghosthomegirls.com/more-about-me. Accessed 7 Jan 2019.

dedMazay. "Donkey carries a large bag, raster." *Shutterstock*, n.d., https://www.shutterstock.com/image-illustration/donkey-carries-large-bag-raster-89568121?src=f5ucbaaXfxa_ysA9-va-JrQ-1-19. Accessed 14 Apr 2019

Ekman, Paul. "Micro Expressions." *Paul Ekman Group*, https://www.paulekman.com/resources/micro-expressions/. Accessed 12 Mar 2019.

Emamzadeh, Arash. "The Cycle of Anger in Relationships." *Psychology Today*, https://www.psychologytoday.com/us/blog/finding-new-home/201901/the-cycle-anger-in-relationships?amp. Accessed 14 Mar 2019.

English Standard Version. Bible Gateway, https://www.biblegateway.com/versions/English-Standard-Version-ESV-Bible/. Accessed 17 Mar 2019.

"Id." *Collegiate Dictionary. Merriam-Webster*, 2019, https://www.merriam-webster.com/dictionary/id.

Jacobs, Martha. "Judges 4:4–10, 12–16, John 4:1–30, 39–42." 15 Mar 2015, First Congregational Church. Sermon.

King James Version. Bible Gateway, https://www.biblegateway.com/versions/King-James-Version-KJV-Bible/. Accessed 13 Jan 2019.

Liu, Jie, et al. "Mutual Cyclical Anger in Romantic Relationships: Moderation by Agreeableness and Commitment." *Journal of Research in Personality*, *77*, pp 1–10. DOI: 10.1016/j.jrp.2018.09.002

Mayo Clinic Staff. "Germs: Understand and protect against bacteria, viruses, and infection." *Mayo Clinic*, https://www.mayoclinic.org/diseases-conditions/infectious-diseases/in-depth/germs/art-20045289. Accessed 10 May 2019.

New International Version. Bible Gateway, https://www.biblegateway.com/versions/New-International-Version-NIV-Bible/. Accessed 17 Jan 2019.

New Living Translation. Bible Gateway, https://www.biblegateway.com/versions/New-Living-Translation-NLT-Bible/. Accessed 21 Jan 2019.

"Overview of Learning Styles." Learning-styles-online, https://www.learning-styles-online.com/overview/. Accessed 14 Mar 2019.

Patton, Stacey. "Stop Beating Black Children." *The New York Times*, 12 Mar 2017, p. SR10.

"Perishable." *Collegiate Dictionary. Merriam-Webster*, 2019, https://www.merriam-webster.com/dictionary/perishable.

Princeton University. "Choosing Your Communication Style." U Matter: Actively Caring for Yourself and Others, https://umatter.princeton.edu/respect/tools/communication-styles. Accessed 21 Apr 2019.

Psychology Today Posted Jun 25, 2016 "These Are the 7 Types of Love...and how we can ignore the most available and potentially fulfilling types." Author Neel Burton M.D

"Retard". *Collegiate Dictionary. Merriam-Webster*, 2019, https://www.merriam-webster.com/dictionary/retard.

Richmond, Raymond. "Boundaries." A Guide to Psychology and its Practice, http://www.guidetopsychology.com/boundaries.htm. Accessed 24 Mar 2019.

Sheppard, Tony L. *Parent Guide to the Anger Thermometer & the Anger Rules*. Groupworks, Incorporated, 2016.

Skiba, Richard. "Code Switching as a Countenance of Language Interference." *The Internet TESL Journal*, vol. 3, no. 10, Oct 1997. http://iteslj.org/Articles/Skiba-CodeSwitching.html.

Smeitana, B. "Lifeway Research: Americans are Fond of the Bible, Don't Actually Read It." Lifeway, 25 April 2017, https://lifewayresearch.com/2017/04/25/lifeway-research-americans-are-fond-of-the-bible-dont-actually-read-it/. Accessed 24 Feb 2019.

Stetzer, E. "New Research: Less than 20% of Churchgoers Read the Bible Daily. Christianity Today, 13 September 2012, https://www.christianitytoday.com/edstetzer/2012/september/new-research-less-than-20-of-churchgoers-read-bible-daily.html. Accessed 25 Feb 2019.

Substance Abuse and Mental Health Services Administration. *Anger Management for Substance Abuse and Mental Health Clients: Participant Workbook*. HHS Pub. No. (SMA) 12-42210. Rockville, MD: Center for Substance Abuse Treatment, 2002.

Tim's Printables. "Maslow's Hierarchy of Needs." https://www.timvandevall.com/printables/maslows-hierarchy-of-needs/. Accessed 15 May 2019.

"Violation." *Oxford Thesaurus*, 2019, https://en.oxforddictionaries.com/thesaurus/violation.

Wine, E. Faye. "Putting it all together." *Agenda: Chosen Jewels*, 1st Books Library, 2002.

Woodward, Orrin. "Orrin Woodward Quotes." Goodreads, https://www.goodreads.com/quotes/870106-learn-to-use-the-criticism-as-fuel-and-you-will. Accessed 16 May 2019.

ABOUT THE AUTHOR

Hey, sisters!

Just a little about me. I am Dr. Antionette D. Brookins a.k.a. Lady Nett, licensed marriage and family therapist, PhD in Christian Psychology. I am an ordinary woman with an extraordinary heart for God's people.

God has blessed me to use my testimony of hurt and healing to compel other women to let go of their debilitating past and walk in the fullness of joy—a joy that only a relationship with our Heavenly Father can bring.

With a unique style, an infectious sense of humor, and God's strength, I use extensive training coupled with practical faith-based counseling techniques to empower, educate, and counsel women from all walks of life.

I am a senior pastor's wife, a mother, grandmother, aspiring author, and successful business owner. HolyGhost HomeGirls, LLC, Antionette Brookins & Associates Family Counseling Corp, a group psychotherapy practice where I have six on staff and founder and clinical director of Destination.Hope Counseling & Enrichment Center, a 501c3 organization.

Just a plain ol' girl from the hood of Fresno who decided to take a leap of faith—and God caught me!

CPSIA information can be obtained
at www.ICGtesting.com
Printed in the USA
LVHW010831260420
654459LV00004B/702